MW00398996

THE PINK NECTAR CAFÉ

Cindy Perin

THE PINK NECTAR CAFÉ

MYTHS AND MYSTERIES

JAMES BISHOP, JR.

WILDCAT PUBLISHING ■ SKULL VALLEY, ARIZONA

The Pink Nectar Café: Myths and Mysteries
Copyright ©2011 by James Bishop, Jr. All rights reserved.

No part of this book may be reproduced or transmitted in
any form or by any means, electronic or mechanical, including
photocopying, recording or by any information storage and retrieval
system, without written permission of the author. For requests
to use any part of this book, please contact: bishop@esedona.net.

Published by Wildcat Publishing, Skull Valley, AZ

Printed in the United States.
Cover and book design: Jane Perini
www.thundermountaindesign.com
Photography: Wib Middleton, pages 100, 106

ISBN: 978-0-615-52675-1
First printing, August 2011

DEDICATION

*To the men and women who've crossed my path
and left their mark, especially Amie, Jeb and Bill.*

ACKNOWLEDGMENTS

Many people helped to bring this book to life, whether it was by the stories they told, the hikes we shared, the books we read or the Pinot Noir sipped by the light of a desert moon. Boatmen and bartenders, teachers and artists, gardeners and politicians, lovely ladies and rumpled cowboys, screenwriters and surfers, they gave me the courage, strength, humor and the hope to carry it on. In common, we shared Rudyard Kipling's rules for writers—or anyone else—in need of tips to be guided through life: "What and Why and When and How and Where and Who."

Salutations go to Jack Proctor, Chip Davis, Steve Ayres, Dan Campbell, Lorena Williams, Thom Stanley, Lisa Heidinger, Eric Glomski, Wib Middleton, JoAnn Olson, Sally Stryker, Joe Neri, Samantha Ruckman, Diane Dearmore, Holly Shannon, Holly Forsman, Ellie Harris, the cowboy/bartender, Jay, and the spirits of Alan Caillou, Morrie Horowitz and Doug Rigby.

Truth be revealed, there'd be no book at all without the inspiration and experience of grammatically erudite Bennie Blake, top editor, and the dedication of Jane Perini, gifted book designer and graphic artist.

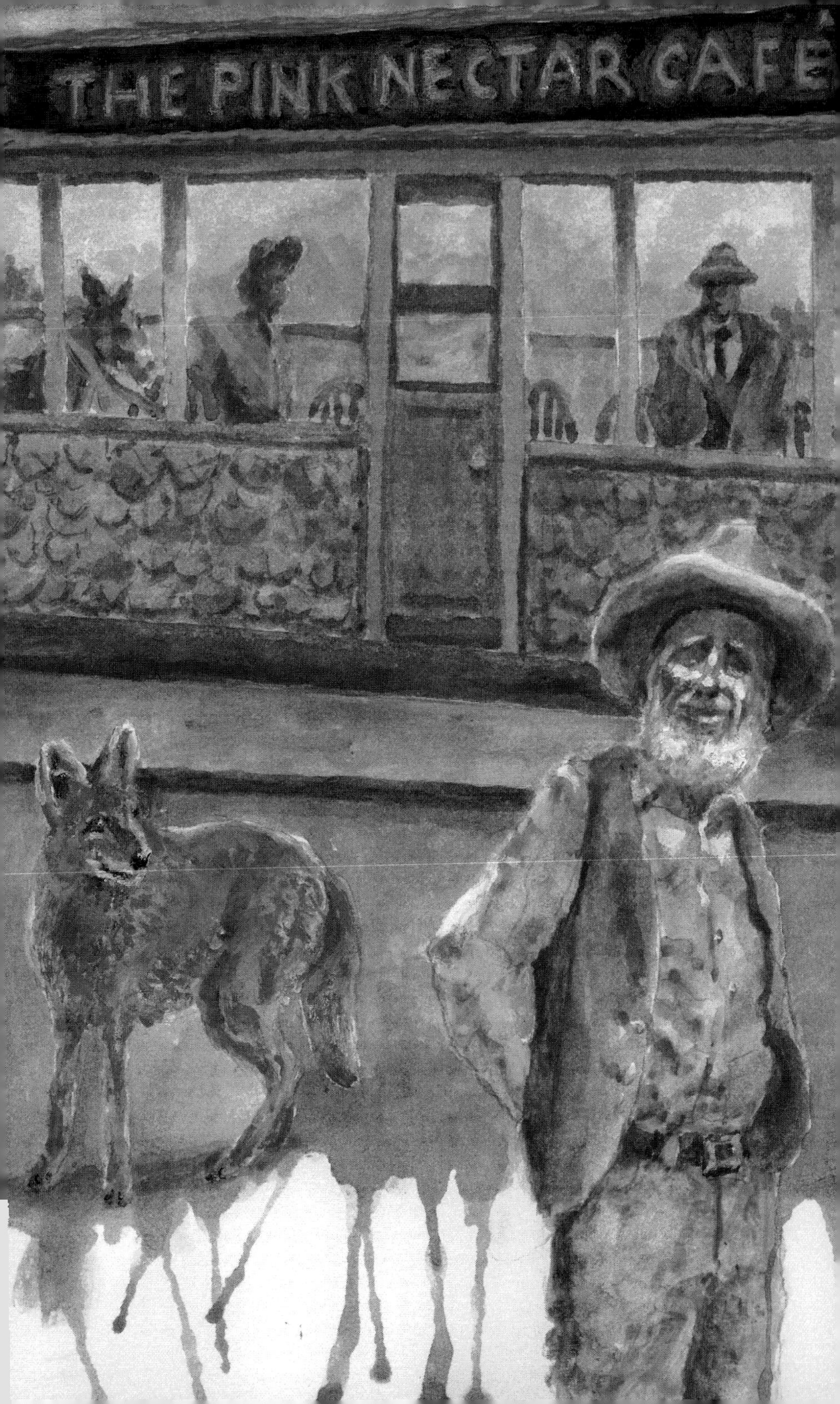
THE PINK NECTAR CAFÉ

CONTENTS

Everybody's wondering what and where
they all came from. Everybody is worried 'bout
where they're all going to go when the whole thing's done.
No one knows for certain so if it's all the same to me,
I think I'll just let the mystery be.

- IRIS DEMENT

Without mystery, life shrinks. The completely known
is numbing void to all active minds.

- EDWARD O. WILSON

PREFACE

his book resting in your hand is a collection of stories. Even better than that, it's a collection of mystery stories. The book itself, and how it came to be, is a mystery. It is made up of tales, some from ancient times, others from only yesterday. They are all true. Some pursued author James Bishop, Jr., for more than 20 years, and all together, they found a home in his head and heart, there to stay. Accepting the tantalizing challenge of the unknown and intrigued by what he could not explain, he began to write. This volume is the result.

Here, the author makes no attempt to solve the mysteries or to take the mystery out of these strange events. He merely leaves his reader free to imagine and to explore the unknown, even beyond these pages. He just lets the mystery be.

Using his artistry with words, Bishop captures the attention, weaves the mystery and leaves his reader free to celebrate its creative energy.

So, now it's time to sink down into a favorite, comfortable chair and get ready for a good read and a journey into the unknown.

- BENNIE BLAKE, AUTHOR, EDITOR, PROFESSOR

INTRODUCTION

n his autobiography, *All the Strange Hours*, anthropologist Loren Eiseley recalls his days as a drifter back in the 1930s. One chilly September evening, in a hobo camp near a Kansas railroad, he talked for hours around a campfire with a Mexican Indian. Decades have bustled by since I first came upon his description of that meeting. Yet, as I drifted from journalism, to government, to teaching, to writing for film and moved from east to west and back again, I've never forgotten Eiseley's description of that Indian: "He leaned forward out of a dark millennium, fierce, wild, intent, studying my face… behind his pupils glimmered the backbone of the Americas before the Ice Age. The last mammoths were there and the long cold dawn which this man had traveled…naked ice and fire and meat are still there in his face."

To Eiseley, drifters lack real existence because one can't ever be sure whether their sometime companions are from the past or from the future. Such drifters, in his experience, carry in their eyes and speech, glimmers of past adventures, hopes, sorrows and mysteries which have evolved in song, poetry and stories.

Country singer Iris Dement's words "Let the mystery be," inspired me to record some of the uncanny tales I have been collecting in the Southwest. In the face of an excess of virtual reality on television and other electronic media, here are tales of men and women having authentic western experiences that, over a space of twenty years, have fallen into my notebook. They range as far and wide as the stunning southwest landscape itself. What happens when an anthropologist is sickened by a devil wind in Navajo-land? How did the tale of Egyptians in the Grand Canyon come about? What happened when an elk hunter found himself face-to-face with a mountain lion? What is the fate of a dying river upon which millions depend? You will meet the implausible Magician, a 12th century warrior and holy man, and a female gambling addict who kicked the habit in jail—against all odds. Too, there's the saga of the legendary gentlewoman who rescued a museum and of a rare falcon that saved a canyon from developers. Another mystery dwells on why early Pueblo people vanished from a haunted canyon. Finally, you may learn how to find the Pink Nectar Café where life-restoring elixir is served, truth is always spoken and Louis Armstrong is said to blow his horn on weekends.

To be sure, the New West is chockablock with gated time-shares, shopping malls and golf courses instead of cattle drives and cowboys; pricey espresso cafés and boutiques instead of down and dirty saloons. No matter, the sheer scale of the open West with its harsh canyon walls, spooky mountains and haunted rivers will always be creating mysteries—such as the Pink Nectar Café. Despite rapid urbanization the region remains linked by myths, legends and stories, and the colors of the primordial landscape, particularly in northern Arizona and southern Utah. They still stir the soul as do the legends of the hardy people who lived there 25,000 years ago. Often, D.H. Lawrence's

words penned long ago in New Mexico resonate in my heart: "...
the moment I saw the brilliant, proud morning shine high up
over the deserts..., something stood still in my soul, and I started
to attend."

Cities are gobbling up the desert, water supplies are being
threatened and clouds of pollution are poisoning air above most
cities. Yet, one may still be stunned by the sudden manifesta-
tion of double rainbows and light playing on towering red rock
formations and the drumming of the hellfire desert sun. There,
you may still meet authentic characters, prehistoric ruins, con-
dors and rivers amidst the red and purple mystery of the Red
Rock Rim Country. They are still there and should be protected,
instead of being valued solely for exploitation.

It struck me, like a glorious monsoon storm that, after all
my years in New York, Washington, D.C. and California, I never knew before what the word "beautiful" truly meant or felt
like. What I've learned over two decades is that landscapes, rivers, ancient ruins, canyons and people can be beautiful if you
love them, if they touch your soul. I know about places between
cities and wilderness where people can live without regret and
which remain unscathed by our destructive interventions, and
I know people who can break your heart. Some of them, even if
long gone, live here in these pages.

- JAMES BISHOP, JR.

The Magician

There are more things in heaven and earth, Horatio,
than are dreamt of in your philosophy.

- WILLIAM SHAKESPEARE

t was the celebrated historian and art critic John C. Van Dyke writing in the 1890s, who was the first to describe the Southwest's arid deserts as both beautiful and precious. Wandering around with a fox terrier and a tough Navajo guide, he discovered another quality, as well: "Look out from the mountain's edge once more...the glory of the wilderness has gone down with the sun. Mystery, that haunting sense of the unknown, is all that remains."

Speaking of mystery, June 25th, 1998, at 10:35 pm Mountain Time, something inexplicable occurred not far from Flagstaff, Arizona. No lucid explanation exists. Several soaring spheres, glowing red to yellow, circled over an excavated prehistoric ruin, hovered, and then landed briefly, leaving never before observed geometric patterns in the volcanic sands. Abruptly, according to eyewitnesses, two veteran U.S. Forest Service Rangers, the spheres climbed out above the ruin, settled into a tight formation and wheeled away to the prehistoric Hopi Indian mesas to the Northeast. A camper later told the local newspaper that he'd seen the vehicles, too.

Where did they come from?

What were they looking for?

Was it something or somebody?

This tale first came to light just before World War II, when archaeologists exploring in that same area stumbled upon the burial site of a large man, close to six feet tall. To put it mildly, there was nothing commonplace about their findings. Buried with the man around 1200 A.D. were 25 whole pottery vessels painted with never before catalogued abstract images, more than 600 other artifacts including shell and stone jewelry, turquoise mosaics, woven baskets, wooden wands, arrow points, beaded wands with carved hands, burial mats, macaws and a beaded skull cap. All together the findings were of such fine workmanship, announced scientist John McGregor at a meeting of the American Philosophical Society meeting in 1943, that "This is the richest burial ever reported in the Southwest."

Leading the list of artifacts was the beaded skullcap, decorated with 3600 beads with holes so tiny, *Arizona Highways* magazine once recorded, that commercial needles available in 1939 couldn't pass through them. The skullcap was pointed, thus the name the Magician.

Most curious was the Magician's facial structure which, according to those who have seen his remains, now locked in a museum's secret vault, did not resemble the facial structure of any of the two dozen different tribal cultures in Arizona. Indeed, some say his face looked to be along European lines.

Theories still fill the air in academe. Was he a Hopi warrior of a now vanished secret clan, who swallowed flaming sticks to frighten intruders? No, say other academics I interviewed, he was a high religious leader possessed with vast sacred power, who died when it was decided that his power should not be passed down to new generations. Did he die a natural death, or was he killed?

This mystery deepened still further when a law went into effect in 1990, the Native American Graves Protection and Repatriation Act. It called for Native American remains, funerary objects, and sacred objects currently in museums to be returned, if asked, to the particular tribe and reservation from whence they came. When numerous scientists asked Hopi tribal elders who'd seen the remains to take the Magician off their hands at the museum, they swiftly backpedaled, shaking their heads no, according to knowledgeable scientists.

So who was the Magician? That mystery was buried along with him. But there's one more thing. It was over the Magician's burial site that the mysterious spheres hovered, and then vanished. Was it their way of paying respect? Or was this event a mysterious expression of awe at something as yet beyond the reach of human knowledge, our dreams, and our philosophy?

The mystery endures. Perhaps Shakespeare had it right when he penned Hamlet's words: "There are more things, Horatio…."

Let the mystery be!

The Pink Nectar Café

A coffin on wheels is her bed
At five in the afternoon
Bones and flutes resound in her ears
At five in the afternoon

- Federico Garcia Lorca

"Do you hear them?" Her voice was drifting away to a whisper at the same time as a welcoming ocean breeze floated through the bedroom of her adobe home above the Pacific Ocean near Malibu Beach. My mother was gripping a book of Vincent Millay's poems in her right hand; nothing odd about any of that on California afternoons in the summertime. She loved reading poetry and falling into a nap. Yet there was something different about this afternoon. She wasn't just napping. For the first time, there were her murmurs.

"I see painted horses on the walls...where will you go...? Arizona? Too late for here!"

My thoughts were scattered. What does one say to a cancer-riddled mother; her physician in Santa Monica had said she could still pull through. Just then, such hopeful thoughts were interrupted by the thud of a burly grey owl landing on the window sill of the casement window near her bed, its talons scratching frenetically at the glass in the partly opened window.

"Just saying goodbye, I guess," she whispered as she adjusted an oxygen hose and shudders of pain shook her dwindling body. "Under the bed…some pills in a wooden box. If it gets… will you help me… you know…on my way?" Lord have mercy, it never came to that. To this day, I don't think I could have done what she wished. Now she wanted to rest. As I had been doing for weeks, I checked to make sure that the oxygen machine that was prolonging her life was working as it should, and then this ever so weary oldest son lay down on the floor next to her bed and pulled a red woolen Indian blanket over his legs.

Now her murmurs were becoming whispers. This onetime fashion model; celebrated artist; three-time wife; friend to both the famous and the lowly, Dukes and gardeners, was prattling about "two boys splashing in the pond…white horses are galloping across the green meadow, heading toward a bright, blue light." Suddenly, with a gasp and a shudder, the machine began to slow down. Just then the machine rasped, rattled and stopped. The patient was beyond oxygen. The Bird of Passage, the name she gave herself in her diary, had flown. So had a cloud of owls perched in the nearby eucalyptus tree. No one in the neighborhood had ever seen so many owls before.

A week later, her cremated remains were dropped into the ocean near Catalina Island, at a spot where the family once fished. Deep in icy waters she may be, never far from memories of those who admired and loved her, as forever looms nearer and nearer for them. The Millay line she was reading before the end was this one: "I only know that summer sang in me a little while, that in me sings no more."

Inside the wobbly airport van, drops of sweat dribbled down the driver's weathered pock-marked red face, sometimes pausing to rest on his bulbous red nose, jarringly reminiscent of actor W. C. Field's, only to be swept away by the brush of a free hand. Every few minutes, he'd mumble some words, tourist chatter like "Arizona is where hell spends the summer." The other passenger was a freckle-faced woman just this side of middle age. Even though the temperature must have been close to 100 degrees, she was wrapped in a thick purple woolen sweater. On her head was a black woolen hat. As a way to while away the time on our two-hour drive north to Arizona's Verde Valley— and little known Sedona then—from the Phoenix Airport, she toyed with a map, and flirted with the driver. I was trying to bury myself in some of my late mother's papers when the lady interrupted me in a voice one might describe as Long Island lockjaw.

"Excuse me, sir, perhaps you can tell me? Where I can find the Pink Nectar Café? I hear from my psychic that a magical drink is served there, able to heal the mind, body and spirit."

Sometimes it makes no sense to get out of bed in the morning. Here I was in the Red Rock Rim landscape Zane Grey made famous in the early part of the 20th century, the land the 16th century Spanish called the Northern Mystery, looking for my old friend Nugent's ex-wife in some place called Sedona and feeling waves of grief.

A new adventure was the last thing I needed on that sizzling

August day and no rain in sight. The sun was relentlessly hammering our creaking old van, so that it felt like the Devil's kitchen on wheels—and the air outside and inside was 99 degrees and climbing, the driver needlessly insisted on informing us.

Never heard of such a place, I told her, besides I'd seen no mention of it in the AAA guide that I'd studied on the jetliner flight from LA. Still, I began to wonder whether such a place could exist. No doubt about it, I was then as innocent about local superstitions and mysteries as a cloistered nun. During my wanderings, I'd read some Stegner, D.H. Lawrence, Mary Austin, and some dramatic ranting by an author by the name of Edward Abbey. Clearly, no other region in America abounded with as many myths except perhaps Robert Service's Yukon where "strange things are done in the midnight sun," indeed. Come to think of it, what I wouldn't mind was a friendly saloon where I might gather my wits with the help of an adult beverage, and think of some way to save my mother's house above the Pacific from the IRS; yes, that was it, a good, old-fashioned saloon like the ones I'd left behind in North Hollywood and Washington, D.C.—The Class Reunion and The Cock and Bull.

Once again, my mental meanderings were interrupted by the lady in the heavy sweater. Could I help her? What did I know about that café? Instead, to be polite I asked her who she was. To this day, I recall her very words: "I am married to an oil tycoon in Texas. I have been wandering here and there in search of who I really am. It was in North Hollywood that I found the key."

"The key to what?" I asked. She explained that her special psychic spoke of a place in the rocks and canyons around Sedona, where there is a combination saloon, bed and breakfast, UFO landing site and New Age meditation compound. "From behind the bar made of turquoise," my new companion related with a gleam in her eye, "a lady by the name of Aurora serves up a special, sweet-tasting drink; pink, life-giving nectar of some sort—or so I am told. Hope it's true, don't you?"

Hmmmmmmm! Interesting details. Might there be such a place? I pressed on for more. She went on to reveal that, when one quaffs even a drop of the pink nectar, sexual drive is re-stored, wrinkles disappear and the brain sweeps away all nega-tive thoughts and feelings and euphoria reigns.

As she talked on and on, memories of my mother's death fell away for the first time in weeks. Soon my van-mate was talk-ing about the different levels of consciousness that one may dis-cover if one spends a few days around the café's underground caves where warm, salty lagoons flow—at least eight different levels, she'd been told by the California psychic.

Okay, now I was paying attention. As the van rolled into a dusty town, I asked her what people did at the café for fun, apart from rediscovering their sexual prowess, or discovered it for the first time. Without any hesitation she said she'd heard that Louis Armstrong plays there in the main ballroom every other Saturday and the lecture series features Joe Namath and Geronimo.

Well, that was that. I knew then that this lady was going through life with just one oar in the water. Geronimo has been dead for more than 100 years, Namath can barely walk, and as for Louis, well now he plays with the angels. Our conversa-tion ended when the battered bus clunked to a stop in front of a grimy-looking saloon named the Wrenwood Café. "Welcome to Sedona," said the driver, "land of the fruits, nuts and woo-woos." We all said goodbye, and for fun I wished the lady luck in finding that magical café, even though I figured she had as much chance as a man fighting a forest fire with snowballs.

At that point, a plumpish, roundish little man sporting a sullied white beard sauntered up and asked whether I needed any help, and then he offered to purchase a beverage for me inside the smoky saloon. His beverage of choice was a Bombay Gin Martini—ice cold and straight up. He said his name was Morrie, and he needed a drink because he'd just fired his senior staffer, Ranger Bob, for insubordination at his world-renowned, underground paper, the *Excentric.*

At his suggestion, my concoction was what was called a Gila monster—part tequila and part grapefruit juice, brew of the ancient gods, he said. After draining his copper goblet, my host, who noticeably hadn't bathed in a while, asked me where I was staying. I told him that I was looking for someone and I might be in town for a day or two or longer. Just couldn't say right away.

"Whatever, young man, come hither and thither with me," he mumbled under the full weight of the Bombay beverage. "The Pink Nectar Café has rooms and the music to be played tonight is tops—Billy Holiday will be singing. Come on along, I'll drive you out there. It's just beyond the back of beyond. And don't worry about paying. I know the owner, you see. One word of advice, now that you're in the New West and bound to rent a car and meet some ladies: if it has tits or wheels, you're going to have trouble down the line."

I thanked him for the invite but told him I wasn't ready to go to the café yet, and he walked away; at the moment I had some memories to deal with. My brain felt like a New England stuffed attic in which pictures from my mother's last moments were stored and needed to be brought forth to be magnified or reduced in order to deal with the sorrow which flowed within me—sorrow not for her but for days together we never had. Sitting at the bar full of dusty cowboys and women with feathered boas wrapped around them, with the music of the Eagles shaking the juke box, I ordered another cocktail, another house special, A Mexican Firing Squad, and drifted back in a dream state to the hours after she passed away.

I was walking on a trail in the Santa Monica Mountains high above her house. A half-moon hung like a sliver of gold over the ocean. The heavens were ablaze with planets and stars. Above me, I saw a new constellation; in its anthropomorphic shape it was a dead ringer for my mother's favorite art piece she titled the Feather Man, a prehistoric shape-shifting shaman she created of bones, sticks and owl feathers.

Both joy and relief filled me, too, for the very heavens had welcomed one of her creations, a fascinating channel for the creative fury in her veins in which flowed the blood of unarmed French Huguenots that surged in the streets of Paris on August 24, 1572—more than 100,000 of them, slain by the soldiers of the Roman Catholic clergy.

It was said that the rivers of France were so filled with corpses that for many months no fish were eaten. In the valley of the Loire, wolves came down from the hills to feed upon the decaying bodies of the French Protestants. The Brokaws, our antecedents, escaped somehow to Holland and then to Long Island in the late 1600s.

Who will remember my mother, Lucile Brokaw, after I have left the planet, too? What will our lives have meant, after all?

At first light, the day after she passed, I awoke and looked out the window to enjoy a cloud-splattered indigo sky, too early for dirty brown LA pollution to creep like a noxious haze from downtown to Santa Monica state beach. She was gone. Just like that, the thin veil between this world and the other had been pierced. The moment I had dreaded, those seconds when what the imagination churns up becomes real, was at hand: The invincible spirit and celebrated artist, a true bird of passage who came to believe in the unseen, had flown away for good. There'd be no more long-distance phone calls to her from the places my work took me—China, Saudi Arabia, Brussels; no more talk of the beauty of the orange nasturtiums in the greenhouse, the orchids in the patio, or what an abysmal new art critic was writing about her art for the *Los Angeles Times*.

Now, only a few owls remained in the trees above the old house. Were they there to watch over me? How much do they know? Still at the bar, I remembered that, two weeks after she died, trying to shake off the guilt of not having been at her bedside sooner, I found myself wandering around in a supermarket in Santa Monica, determined to be alone with my grief. As I went down the aisle to a sign that read that good rum was on sale, a grey-haired woman with an aquiline nose, dangling silver earrings and draped in a purple shawl approached.

"Excuse me but I know you. You're her son, aren't you? She showed me your picture." The woman looked somehow familiar, she was friendly enough; yet I couldn't place her. She spoke softly again. "You see, I collected her art and we were friends, too. Did you know that she gave many things away when she knew she couldn't hang on much longer, she gave away her Macaws and the big desert turtle?" I knew no such thing for she had concealed her illness from the rest of the family until nearly the end.

Memories flooded back. "How is the old turtle?" I asked, recalling how my daughter, Amie, had loved to feed it with nasturtiums.

"He left the planet the same day she did, just stopped breathing. I know it was the same day because I read her obit in the *Los Angeles Times*. You know, desert turtles like hers live for hundreds of years. There was nothing wrong with old 'Turt', as she called him. Perhaps he decided to go with her; you know how she believed in the mysterious—spirits and the like, things didn't have to be seen to be believed. Did you know much about her art?" I said that I had been to some of her shows, but none lately. "Well, let me tell you, young man. She was a master of a different kind of art, a much older art, that of the image maker, the idol maker. It is medicine man craft, dispenser of luck and special powers. She dispelled the dullness in the world."

I nodded politely, thanked her and walked away, wondering what to make of her story. Mother had never talked to me about what her art was all about.

A few days later, I fell asleep on a couch on her patio and was quickly ferried into dreamland, helped by the aromas arising from a cluster of gardenia plants nearby. There I was standing in a cavernous, shadowy hall, that felt like some sort of gymnasium. Not far away, I saw my mother climbing a spiral staircase. Wrapped in a luminous gown, she turned her head a few times to glance at me. God, she was winking at me just like she always did. Just ahead of her at the top stood a group of people in white hospital tunics; they were extending their hands as if to welcome her and to encourage her to keep climbing.

Beyond them, she could see a crowd of others who were

also waving her on—her two husbands, two sisters and her mother. With a wave at me, she disappeared into the light. Awake now, I felt a huge surge of relief. The dream was her farewell gift. Although her ashes were now food for the fish off Catalina Island, her spirit was safe with people who loved her when she was alive. Was that dream truly created by my own imagination, or had she sent it to me?

Now, more than twenty years later, I am filled with wonder and mystery about my departed mother. The memories, the dreams and the chance encounter at the California supermarket are with me still. I realize my future has sprung from those memories—love of the arts, fighting for wild nature, the heavens and stories that glue our culture together, always resisting the inducement to despair about what Man has done to the Earth. These days, I live near that creek in Sedona where she thought I'd belong—waiting for the owls. I still wonder why she hadn't gone to an oncologist sooner. Or, was it just her time to go?

Let the mystery be!

Wicked Navajo Winds

Life is the continual intervention of the inexplicable.

- ERWIN CHARGAFF

a s a Washington correspondent for a national magazine
in the '60s and '70s, one constant was changing hour-
ly deadlines and pursuing tips about the next scan-
dal. Now that I have settled in the Southwest, challenges have
changed and one in particular surely would have been labeled as
ludicrous by former colleagues: to drive across the vast Navajo
Reservation in Utah, New Mexico, and Arizona, an area the size
of New England, trying to forget the challenging warnings given
to me by tribal elders.

They said to beware of deadly dust-devil winds and bizarre
rock formations on both sides of the highway, these having been
placed there by the Holy Mist People, and the Monster Slayer.
This other-worldly creature is celebrated in Navajo mythology
for ambushing the chief of the enemy gods, whose blood became a massive lava flow still seen today along main highways
in Arizona and New Mexico.

Such bizarre fears were never mine when I was covering

Watergate, environmental and energy policy; had someone told me about the Navajo myth then, I would have dismissed it as idiotic fantasy. But that was no longer the case, once I'd met David by accident one evening at a gathering of freelance writers on a ranch on the outskirts of Flagstaff, Arizona.

Off in a corner and away from the boozy crowd, a swarthy academic with piercing dark eyes was telling a story to a red-haired woman, my date for the night. I could see that he was fidgeting as she confided to him, as she did to everyone, that she was always being attacked by helicopter gods in the form of horny men and priests. As I joined them, he was telling her a tale that made me forget all about helicopter gods. After hearing some of the details, I had to find out much more, so I made an appointment to meet him for coffee at a local joint, in a small café near the railroad. At first we made small talk about writers, wine and women. When I told him that I wished to write something, he said sure but I was not to use his name. Then he jumped right in by informing me that his midnight dreams about huge gargoyles with burning red eyes and seaweed for nostril hair had finally ceased. For the first time in weeks he was back at his desk at the university, and he was sleeping again. However, said he, he was not the same man, or the same scientist that he'd been only a month before—and never would be, again.

By an accident of fate he'd wandered into a nonscientific realm, into a dimension which European scientists refuse to acknowledge. Yet, because of an inexplicable experience, he was on the verge of abandoning a promising career in anthropology. He'd recognized just how little outsiders knew about what really happens in the Navajo culture. As testament to that realization, he pinned some words from *Hamlet* to the wall above his desk at Northern Arizona University: "There are more things in heaven and earth, Horatio, than are dreamt of in your philosophy." Until recently, he had paid little or no attention to other things "in heaven and earth," since they were not contained in his anthropological text books—all of which dismissed anything supernatural.

In Edward Abbey's *The Brave Cowboy* the valley and the mountains and the silent desert are haunted—"troubled, vexed, by ghosts, phantoms, and vagrant spirits. You can hear them down along the river, shaking and whispering in the leaves of the old cottonwoods."

My new friend David said that, while he'd enjoyed Ed Abbey's writing, all that stuff about phantoms and spirits to him was nonsense. "I was trained not to believe in the supernatural," he asserted when the subject came up about his ethnographic field activities. Simply stated, his work for the Navajo government included recording historic sites and gravesites, preparatory to road-building projects on tribal lands in Arizona, New Mexico and Utah, and that was that.

Despite his denial of anything supernatural, he was nonetheless well informed about the creation stories celebrated by the various tribes that hired him for his professional experience. He understood that, according to the Navajo creation story, beyond the measurement of time, the Dineh or "the people" as they call themselves, lived in the first world, the Black World. The Dineh took the form of Holy Mist beings, and they did not live in harmony with each other or with their environment.

According to oral history, they were soon banished and forced to move into the second world, the Blue World. They didn't stay there long, either, because they refused to adhere to ethical principles and had to move once more, this time into the third world, called the Glittering World, the one in which they live today. Eons ago they'd promised the gods they'd live in harmony with everything—the plants, animals, insects, mountains, trees and all living things. They promised to treat the Earth as their mother, the sky as their father, and from childhood they were weaned on stories about Spider Woman, whose web, when she threw it high into the air, became all the stars in the sky.

David respected the Navajo for their creation stories, but these had nothing to do with the rigid scientific tenets of anthropology that guided his work. At the top of his list was the tale of a dusty whirlwind the Navajo call chindi, spawned by evil deities who suck the wind from the person, their very breath of life, as punishment for living in the wrong way. What is more, the wind sucked from the dead person doesn't just blow away. It becomes the dreaded chindi which, if it blows in a counter-clockwise direction, can make people very sick. The Navajo do many things to avoid the chindi, the evil wind. It is believed that certain places, certain rocks, certain canyons are sources of chindi; thus, many Navajos avoid those places.

To avoid this evil wind, Navajos will carry relatives near death to the side of a road, far from their traditional dwelling, the hogan. There they'll lay them down in hopes that a passing tourist will pick them up and rush them to a hospital. If someone dies in the hogan, it will be burnt to the ground in order to destroy the evil wind. Down through the years, David had chalked up such stories as supernatural fantasy. Before long, however, David found himself in the center of one of those very fantasies, only it was all too real.

And it all had begun so routinely, another project, another

paycheck, just another week of work on the Navajo reservation. According to his contract with the Navajo government, he and his partner Hawk, a Navajo, were to research areas on both sides of a proposed road leading from Tuba City, Arizona, to a two-lane highway. They were tasked to catalogue sites used historically for religious ceremonies; all in all it appeared to be an everyday assignment for this experienced team.

Together, they divided up the task. David, in his careful scientific way, was to interview tribal elders and record the sites that might be threatened by bulldozers and road-scrapers. Meantime, Hawk would interview local residents and gather data on special sites, such as ancient burial mounds. Also, they focused their attention on one particular elder, a healer or a medicine man called Gray Clouds. They'd been told by other elders that he had the greatest knowledge of the area; too old to walk, it was said, but he liked to talk.

On their first day outside Tuba City, they were driving along in the high desert on a narrow, dusty road when David became a bit irritated upon hearing the old Navajo man conversing with Hawk in the Navajo tongue. But then he relaxed, knowing that his partner would share any important details with him. Meantime, what startled David was that the old man seemed to have exceptional vision for someone so elderly, maybe close to 100 years old. He kept pointing out rocks, boulders and other special trees and bushes that David himself couldn't see, even with his good vision.

At one place known as Wolf Rock, the old man grew silent as if he was meditating. To David the scene didn't look particularly special or interesting, more like the NASA photos of Mars he'd seen, what with sandstone boulders of all shapes and sizes strewn everywhere, the kind of rocks that scientists call "erratics."

What David did not know, until Hawk told him later, was that the old man was seeing and feeling something else entirely. For that place, he'd told Hawk, was where the Holy Mist people had camped in the earliest times, a thousand years or more ago. Because they were linked to origin stories, it was they, not earthquakes, weather, wind, or volcanic eruptions that had placed the rocks and boulders in their special places. Too, the Holy Mist people knew how to generate a holy wind and had imparted wisdom to the rocks, which is why they were placed together in such perfect balance. Upon hearing that tale, David scoffed, as he usually did, upon hearing tales of the supernatural.

Speaking in Navajo, the old holy man also told Hawk, but forbade him to say anything to David, he later learned, that the place where they were standing was where secret ceremonies were still held: the Night Way, the Blessing Way, the Enemy Way. Such ceremonies were necessary, the elder explained, to remind younger generations in the tribe that they must acknowledge the balance of the rocks, boulders and trees. Such ceremonies were necessary to remind new generations of Navajos that their behavior should mirror that sacred balance at certain times with special prayers and certain chants. Should this not be done, the elder warned, should the holy people not be acknowledged in the established way at the proper times, retribution was inevitable. What was at stake was preserving the spiritual links between the tribal people and the landscape!

It was then that the elder turned on David. Speaking in English, and in an angry tone, he directed a question to David: "How can I answer your questions about whether this tree or that tree should be preserved or not? It is all holy. How can you know these meanings in a few weeks?"

David smiled at the old medicine man and told him respectfully that he and Hawk had no intention of being presumptuous about any aspect of Navajo life and tradition. Over and over again, he repeated that they were working for his government and that their only interest was in identifying the impacts road construction could have on the very land the elder was protecting.

The old man was silent.

Two weeks before their work was due to be completed, David and Hawk took the same elder out for a drive, along with a female scientist who was part-Navajo and part-Anglo and fluent in both languages. After they'd left the town behind, Grey Clouds, the elder, raised his arm as a signal to stop the jeep.

Off to the right, David saw the remains of a sweat lodge and a hogan. At that point, the elder became animated and began chattering in his own language. Then, he turned to the female scientist and raised his voice while gesticulating with his dirt-brown, leathery hands. His voice rose to a high-pitch cry in English, "Take me back, for I am sick."

At the hotel in Tuba City that evening, Hawk told David what had really transpired earlier in the day. Near where they'd parked was a sandstone mound that David had not seen. Grey Clouds had told Hawk that it was a place the Holy People visited long, long ago. Nearby were three upright red rock slabs with a narrow opening; two were perfectly straight; the third was cut off at the top.

In times past, this had been a place for late night offerings and chants. At the bottom of one of those slabs was a large cellar, designated by tradition to be for men only. It turned out that the elder, the medicine man, became incensed that a woman had been with them. She may have heard certain things about the place they were scrutinizing, and he heard her say certain things she never should have said in front of David, an Anglo, an outsider, a white man, a stranger, a possible enemy.

Finally, the elder pleaded with Hawk not to discuss any details about any of that, because certain details were known only to designated medicine men. "Even if that knowledge dies with them," explained Hawk, repeating the elder's words, "it is better to die than allow it to fall into the wrong hands." Then the old man asked to be taken back to his hogan.

With every passing hour, David grew more uncomfortable about working in such an unscientific realm with all the talk of the Holy Wind, the Holy Mist people. This was not what he had earned a Master's degree to do. "Do tribal people tell scientists like me only what they want us to know?" David asked himself one night. "Do they keep their real secrets, especially about certain religious practices, and even die with them so that they are not abused by non-traditional people?"

One more day of work remained, and another Navajo elder, who was reputed to be knowledgeable, agreed to take the two of them out to see some other sites, places with even older stories attached to them. David couldn't wait to get home, back to work and to his small apartment, to the running track where he worked out daily, close to his university office. It was time for him to do a serious reevaluation of his career. He couldn't think of a time when he'd felt more uncomfortable. But there was more to come.

On their way to an odd-looking pile of rocks, the threesome passed what looked like a burial mound. David stopped, poked his cottonwood walking stick into the mound, and asked the

Navajo what the mound had been used for down through the years. It was a fruitless quest. "Don't write anything down about what you see here," the Navajo directed. "You ask too many questions, much of our knowledge will never be given to outsiders. Even if you lived among us for 30 years, you would be seen as an outsider. There are many things that cannot be told."

That night David and his Navajo partner sat down at their motel to sort out their research. Questions filled the air! What about the sites they had seen, which would not be recorded? Was that mound some kind of bone bank? Was it ethical to turn in an impact report to the tribal government with so many pieces missing? Despite their doubts, they had a job to finish, so they cobbled together a draft, mailed it next morning and went their separate ways, David to Flagstaff, Arizona, and Hawk to Chinle, near Canyon de Chelly, also in Arizona.

During his normal lunch break the next day, David went to the university track and, while jogging, promptly collapsed onto the black cinders, scraping his legs until they bled. That night he had the first in a series of the gargoyle dreams. He went to his office in the morning, exhausted. Two days later, he checked on his savings account at the local bank and was told that it was closed. No one at the bank knew why. Later that day, he was notified by mail that his health insurance policy had been cancelled. Later that night, he got a call from San Antonio, reporting that his favorite uncle had been felled by a heart attack and was not expected to live.

Confused, scared, and sleepless, David phoned his partner, but before he could say anything, Hawk unloaded on him: His wife had been suddenly fired from her nursing job. Then one of their children fell down the stairs at school and suffered a serious leg sprain. As for Hawk, his own right arm, which had been healing from a serious gash in a back-hoe accident, suddenly became infected. Then one night, Hawk reported, his healthy uncle was struck down with a heart attack.

"It's the chindi," Hawk said.

"This could never happen to us," David replied. "We are scientists, I don't believe in the chindi."

"We need a singer, a medicine man. I know one," countered Hawk.

"I don't believe in that crap, either," David yelled.

Nonetheless, a day later he received instructions from Hawk as relayed from the singer: Immediately mail to the medicine man a piece of cloth that he wore the day they stopped near the triple burial mound. Next, he was to select a piece of green cloth and drive into the pine forest not far away. There he was to choose a pine tree, about the same age as he was, about 40, select two small branches from the tree and bury the sticks and cloth at the base of the tree, all the while reciting a prayer that was part of his childhood. Thinking the whole exercise ludicrous, David nonetheless did what he was told. He was desperate. He had to try something.

Back at the coffee house in Flagstaff, David finished his tale. "On the second night after I buried the bundle, the nightmares stopped; my insurance and savings accounts went back to normal and I have slept fine ever since. And my uncle has recovered. Whatever you do with my tale," David said to me, "don't tell it to anyone east of Ohio because they'll think you're a whack-job; or that Shakespeare's words, 'What fools these mortals be' strictly apply when it comes to non-Indians being able to understand pre-Columbian, tribal cultures. I am moving on."

A year later David resigned his university position and left behind forever all he thought he knew. In his encounter with the Navajo world few Anglos have been close to, it had become clear to him that he could no longer attend conferences where so many scientists talked about how much they knew about tribal cultures. Perhaps someday, they will face the mysterious, too. As for himself, he'd had enough to last a lifetime.

Let the mystery be!

The Ghostwalker

Then said Po-shai-an-kia to the Mountain Lion,
"Long tail, thou art stout of heart and strong of
will. Therefore give I unto thee and unto thy
children forever the mastership of the gods of
prey, and the guardianship of the great Northern
World (for thy coat is of yellow), that thou guard
from that quarter the coming of evil upon my
children of men, that thou receive in that quarter,
that thou become the father in the North of the
sacred medicine orders all, that thou become
a maker of the paths of men's lives."

- ZUNI LEGEND

igh in the Arizona-New Mexico borderlands my friend
Bobby, a veteran elk hunter, had settled himself into a
grassy lair and was finishing the basic elk routine. He'd
un-slung his pack and his rifle, checked the safety, then covered
his heavy brown boots, legs, jacket and hat with creek water
mixed with clay from a small bottle. He wanted to smell like the
earth itself so that no animal could pick up his scent.

Tall, muscled, a desert aficionado and sporting the curly blonde hair of a California surfer, Bobby regarded himself as the ultimate hunter, his favorite prey being elk, wild turkey and deer. For him it was never the enjoyment of the killing itself as much as it was the ritual of the hunt: establishing the command post and erecting the military-issue canvas tent lent to him by his hunting pal Charlie a Viet Nam vet. Next came the setting of lamps and stoves, chopping fallen pinion and juniper, planning meals and enjoying a beverage or two; all this while looking for elk signs. Then, of course, there was always the worry of being jumped by bears. He'd heard the stories.

Forget the stories! This will be a good hunt, he figured. He'd seen elk signs on the way to his lair, clumps of hide on tree branches, scat droppings, and off in the distance he heard elks bugling. He had five days to bag a bull, and then the permit expired. What he couldn't yet know was that this hunt was going to be as different from his others, as having a woman by your side, or on your side.

Wait a minute! The hairs on his beefy red neck were rising. Did he have uninvited company? Turning his head slowly, this big husky hunter had a sinking spell sort of like the monthly call from his bank telling him there's problem with his account. Stretched out not more than six feet from him was the renowned predator known as cougar, puma, panther, more commonly mountain lion, and to the Zuni tribe, Ghostwalker. Never before, in all the years of hunting in the wilds, had Bobby's heart pounded so hard. Was the hunter being hunted? Why hadn't the beast jumped him?

Until that moment, he'd always felt safe in this high plateau now splotched with early winter snow. Among the magnificent ponderosa pines, decked out in a green and brown camouflage outfit, he was in his element, camouflaged and waiting. Because of so many years of elk hunting, he thought he knew the script. First there'd be the sound of tree limbs cracking in the brush around him. Then he'd catch the blur of an antler through the trees, the first sign of the Rocky Mountain Elk, the noble creature he'd driven hundreds of miles to hunt.

Though his mind was reeling with ideas, with the lion so close, thoughts and questions were downright irrelevant. He felt as if he was going to throw up. Thoughts raced through his mind. He remembered his favorite author Edward Abbey's first encounter with a lion. "We peered at each other through the gloom. Mutual curiosity: I felt more wonder than fear. After a minute or perhaps it was five minutes, I made a move to turn. The lion leapt away."

Bobby's whiskered visitor, however, showed no signs of melting away. He figured that, besides being about nine feet long including tail, the beast likely weighed at least 200 pounds. In a split second, the animal could be on him; that thought caused his own breath to come in short gasps.

But wait a minute! The intruder seemed not to have noticed him. How annoying in some respects, what a relief in others. It was busy surveying the same ridge he was, looming like some regal sculpture in front of an ancient queen's throne, its two front legs stretched out, large pads extended.

What with his weapon, camping gear and his seasoned skills Bobby had always felt that he was top dog in the forest; not anymore. Sure, he'd heard from other hunters that the lion was making a remarkable comeback. Yet he never thought he'd meet one. Few humans had ever seen one up close or heard one approaching—just tracks everywhere, as well as the bones of deer and elk. Observed Ellen Meloy in her superb book, *Eating Stone*, mountain lions are "cryptic stalkers, they shape-shift the colors of desert rock and shrub. They travel widely and show up in places where they weren't."

Suddenly, Bobby was as confused as he was scared. Why didn't the lion, the most alert of all North American predators, acknowledge him? He looked again as the animal scanned the ridge with its yellow eyes, nostrils twitching. The lion's tranquil manner puzzled Bobby. He had heard stories of lion attacks, how they ambush humans from the back and side, and kill by inserting their teeth between the victim's neck vertebrae and severing the spinal chord in half.

But with the beast so close he fought off such thoughts. He felt pains in his gut. Thoughts galloped through his mind. Bobby's whiskered visitor showed no signs of leaving. Having read that a lion lives from feast to famine, he wondered if it had just dined on a coyote, a small bear, a wolf or a deer. If so, why was it hunting elk now? Such questions roiled his brain. In the meantime, it occurred to him that the earth scent he'd applied might be working. Maybe at days end, he'd get back to camp down the mountain after all and tell his hunting buddies quite a story. The hell with them if they didn't believe him.

Waiting for the lion to make a move Bobby took a chance and reached into a pocket for his small point-and-shoot camera. To open the lens cover, he flicked a tiny switch which triggered a sharp whirring sound. Like a lightning flash, the big cat flexed its muscles from whiskers to tail. Chest and legs bulged with sinew. Its long, yellow tongue leapt from its mouth and rolled back in. For all that, even then the lion didn't deign to acknowledge him. Bobby aimed his camera, determined to avoid the lion's eyes, should the regal head turn his way. Just as he was ready to shoot a photo, the lion started to move. Its long tail stretched out from its body and swooped straight up in the air.

Had the creature finally caught the hunter's scent? Without looking back, the big cat lurched off into the brush. Bobby took some photos, but to this day he can barely make out the spooky outlines of the lion's hindquarters in the film's negatives. Ghostwalker was being true to its name.

Bobby knew that he had to get the hell off the mountain. The odds were good that the lion had spotted elk on the ridge and soon the bulls and cows would be crashing down right through his hideout, with the lion close behind.

He'd bet correctly. Within five minutes, two elk cows and a calf hurtled through the trees, stopping only to sniff the place where the lion had rested. Twice, they gave off a timid, fearful sound and were gone. Figuring that a bull elk must be close behind, Bobby shouldered his rifle and gear and headed down the mountain. His only thought was there's a lion out there which has pushed two cows and a calf down the ridge—and I am the prey.

For Bobby, what a bizarre dilemma! Face to face with the Ghostwalker, the expert hunter couldn't kill it. Indeed, that was the last idea on his mind. The animal was too regal, and besides, they were after the same prey.

For thousands of years, the lion was the king of beasts in the high country of the Southwest. Many tribal clans believed that the lion was a Great Shaman, a descendant of totemic ancestors born to signal the wonders about them. Despite rampant urbanization in the Southwest, the lion still reigns.

What of Bobby?

As he has done for nearly two decades, the burly artist/carpenter still prepares for elk season in the late Indian summer days when the nippy winds begin to blow, when the first snow is powdering the ponderosas and junipers, and firewood is being gathered by citizens in the forests. From time to time, he sips a beer, lights a cigar and mulls this mystery: Why didn't the lion tear him to pieces all those years ago?

Sometimes, against all odds, the fates conspire in our favor.

Let the mystery be!

NEMO: Child of the Sun

Say that I starved; that I was lost and weary;
That I was burned and blinded by the desert sun;
Footsore, thirsty, sick with strange diseases;
Lonely and wet and cold, but that I kept my dream.

> - EVERETT RUESS, 1932

reaming comes easy in the Southwest, that region of mountains, rivers and canyons 16th century Spanish invaders called the Northern Mystery. Four hundred years later author Ed Abbey dubbed it "The Dreamland" where mysterious canyons are as deep as four Empire State buildings stacked on top of each other and as wide from rim to rim as Manhattan is long.

When first I arrived in "The Dreamland' after decades in polluted cities, on both coasts, I found myself doing a lot of camping, sleeping and dreaming by rippling rivers like the San Juan in Utah, under a sky full of stars and planets amidst a blanket of black velvet studded with jewels.

It is not too much to say that one of those dreams gave me

new eyes to see the world and to see myself. Now, years later, I can still hear that coyote yelping not far away. Early one desert morning back then, there I was with a blanket over me in a small canyon crowded with prehistoric cliff dwellings. Nearby an elderly man with bushy white hair was stirring something in a clay pot. Seeing that I was nearly awake, he brought me a cup of stew. "You'll need this," he said. "You look like you need this… name is Nemo. Don't see many Anglos here…don't know what year it is, what day. What does it matter anyway?"

Feeling better after the stew, I asked the man whether he ever yearned for company. "Company, you say? I don't need no company. I have Cicero, Twain, Abbey, Marlowe and Whitman. I prefer the saddle to the street car and the star-sprinkled sky to a roof, the obscure and difficult trail leading to the unknown. People think I drowned years ago. I let them think that."

When I was fully awake, I tossed the blanket to the side and stood up to listen to the old man some more. I was alone.

What is imagined is real, I've heard gurus say, and what is real is imagined. When I told Susan Kliewer, the celebrated artist, about that dream a few days later, she blanched and said that I must have been visited by Everett Ruess, the lost artist. She'd heard that it had happened to others. She knew all about him from a book she'd read as a little girl in California. Then she told me to read one of Edward Abbey's poems, and said I'd likely never be the same.

You walked into the radiance of death through
passageways of stillness, stone and light…hunter, brother,
companion of our days,
the blessing which you hunted, hunted, too,

what you were seeking,
this is what found you.

-EDWARD ABBEY, 1983

Nearly 80 years have passed since Everett vanished into the red rock canyon labyrinth south of Escalante, Utah, the spooky region that the Spaniards also called the Despoblado, the howling wilderness. So far as is known, he never lived to see his 21st birthday, March 28, 1935. Here are some thoughts that he left behind: Adventure is for the adventurous. My face is set. I go to make my destiny. May many another youth be inspired to leave the snug safety of his rut and follow fortune to other lands.

In every man there lurks the desire to get away from it all, to escape the din and discord of what is termed civilization, and maybe have an exciting adventure. To imagine desperate adventures, after all, is one of youth's civil liberties. Few dare. Even fewer wander alone on the winds of adventure after abandoning family, then stumble into adventures surpassing wildest fantasies, record it all with brush and pen and then vanish forever into the wild lands of southern Utah.

Near the end of his life, Albert Einstein determined that the most fundamental experience for humans is the mysterious. Among all the mysteries hovering around in the Southwest, Ruess's story survives, despite the passage of years, as one of the most intriguing, thanks to the research of Utah's W. L. Rusho, and some of my own.

To this day, speculation about the fate of the young man the Navajos called "Yabitoch," the good humored one, still hums in the desert air. Not long ago, author/anthropologist Scott Thybony encountered an inscription, etched on the wall of a cave he was exploring near Navajo Mountain: Everett Ruess, 1954. "A casual prank? Well, someone went to lots of trouble," Thybony told me later. "Was it him? Who knows?"

At least once a year someone wanders into Flagstaff, Arizona, to report that the boy's bones have been found. Rumors still fly that he simply ran off to Mexico with a dazzling Navajo woman. Whatever his fate, by some miracle his words have survived: "Nature's impact sometimes is so far beyond my powers to convey that it almost makes me despair."

Refusing to face the possibility that Nemo is gone for good, old desert rats bet he's holed up at Keet Seel or Betatakin, Grand Gulch or Canyon de Chelly. Or perhaps he's crossing Monument Valley with his burros, Pericles and Pegasus. Didn't a Navajo medicine man have a vision of him a few years ago at the foot of Navajo Mountain? "For all we know," mused the late Edward Abbey, "he's still down there somewhere, living on prickly pear and wild onions, communing with the gods of river, canyon and cliff."

Every once in a while, however, something truly bizarre occurs as when a college student from Stamford, Connecticut, wandered into the Northern Arizona University library in Flagstaff, seeking information about Ruess for a college project. From a dusty shelf, he pulled a copy of *On Desert Trails*, a memoir of Everett's life, published in 1940. Believe it or not, out fell postcards written by Everett's father, Christopher, to family members around Christmas, 1935, describing the many fruitless searches for his son. "It was quite a shock," says librarian Dick Quartarolli. "How did those cards get from Lees Ferry, Arizona, to Santa Barbara, California, and back again? Another mystery, I guess."

To poets, adventurers, river boatmen and wilderness guides

the name Ruess, like the smoke of a billowing campfire, summons up visions of sculpted horizons, bursts of green, vermilion, rust and cayenne, rivers, rock, sand and sky in landscapes that tug at the heart. For despite surging growth and increased pressure on the land of the Colorado Plateau, the land's breathtaking beauty remains intact, and will be here, wrote Lawrence Clark Powell, "until there is no longer any heart to break for it."

So just maybe, Everett is still out there playing cards with friends, and painting always. Even if he isn't, his spirit is! Since the time of the Greeks, the passing of young men has intrigued the world. Many countries swirl with such myths; none is more enduring than that of the solitary man determined to achieve a communion with nature so nearly absolute as to be irrevocable. At the age when most young men are in high school, Ruess took that "dark trail," in the direction of myth. Ruess's achievement, Pulitzer Prize-winning author N. Scott Momaday contends, "Is the achievement of myth. The young man's capacity for wonder was very great."

For what was he searching? No doubt it was beauty, the late Wallace Stegner believed, "and he conceived beauty in pretty romantic terms. But if we laugh at Everett Ruess, we shall also have to laugh at poet John Muir, because there was little difference between them except age."

Nowadays people need heroes, and Everett's story is an enduring case. Weary of corruption and sleaze, people are looking for models. By any measure, Everett's life truly constitutes an extraordinary model. Born in Oakland, California, in 1914, Everett was the younger of two sons. His father, Christopher, was a Harvard Divinity School Graduate, a poet and a state official while his mother, Stella, home-schooled her son in poetry and in the arts.

By the time Everett reached the age of 14, he'd already experimented with sketching, clay modeling and woodcarving and was recording his life in a journal. By then, his family had finally settled in California after short periods of residence in Boston, Brooklyn, New Jersey and Indiana. Everett, as a sixteen-year-old, attended Otis Art School and Hollywood High for a time but soon embarked on his first solo trip, hitchhiking and trekking through Yosemite and Big Sur and then to Carmel, California.

While in Carmel, he knocked on a door and boldly introduced himself to the renowned photographer, Edward Weston, who encouraged the youngster's efforts at painting and block printing over a period of months. Everett loved the seacoast, but he yearned for the terra incognita—the harsh trackless deserts and snowcapped peaks of the Southwest.

In January 1931, after receiving a diploma from Hollywood High, he was on the road again, winding his way on foot, burro and horse through the wild lands of Arizona, Utah and Mexico, sometimes traveling 30 miles a day. In those days, the only predictable way across the area was on the Santa Fe Railroad and Route 66. Everett, however, kept to the backcountry, killing rattlesnakes as he went, and eating them, being attacked by bees, fending off scorpions, black widow spiders, surviving quicksand, flash floods, illness, and treacherous sandstone ledges.

Along the trail, he made friends, and enemies, with the "Navvies," his name for the Navajos. One Navajo told him that there were rubies in the ant hills on Navajo land, and he should go there. Another told him that spiders carried ancient stories in their stomachs. In addition, he crossed rhetorical swords with missionaries who tried to convert the young agnostic. "I don't see how any intelligent person can believe anything," he wrote in his journal. Along the way, he decided to call himself Nemo, meaning "no one" after the captain in *20,000 Leagues under the Sea*.

Except for a handful of archaeologists, Anglo traders and Mormon ranchers ringing the Hopi and Navajo Nations, Everett's dreamland was perhaps the most lonely and desolate area anywhere in North America, south of Alaska. Yet his letters and poems reveal that he loved it for the visions waiting in ambush; "Double rainbows, sheer incurving cliffs, breathlessly chiseled and gloriously colored, the lunatic quiver of the coyote, the whiplashes of rain," he wrote, and, "To live is to be happy; to be carefree, to be overwhelmed by the glory of it all."

Sometimes he lacked enough water. Sometimes there was too much. In May 1932, he nearly drowned crossing the Salt River near Phoenix, where wild waters ran chest high on the young man, and he almost lost one of his treasured burros. "I've had some terrific experiences in the wilderness, overpowering, overwhelming," he rejoiced in a letter to a friend. "But then I am always being overwhelmed." All the while, the people he met along the way stuck by him, and often fed him whenever they could, especially Maynard Dixon, the celebrated artist.

Aroused by beauty and facing danger indescribable to most of today's hikers and river boatmen, Everett managed to do a remarkable amount of reading by flashlight: Dostoevsky, Thomas Mann, Emerson, Aristotle, Whitman, Ibsen, The Arabian Nights, Shakespeare's *As You Like It* and Robert Browning. Whenever he ran out of books, his mother would send a new batch to a post office box in Chinle, Arizona, Marble Canyon or Hubbell's Trading Post. In addition, when he was able to

sell one of his block prints, he would send the few dollars home
to his parents. Evidence, too, is that whenever he sold one of his
prints, he'd buy a surprise for Navajo kids. Once, he took a bunch
of them to the Orpheum theatre in Flagstaff to see cowboy films.
"So that's how wranglers dress," he wrote to his father, and then
he and his Navajo pals started dressing like screen cowboys.

If Ruess wasn't able to hustle a good meal of fresh beef and
vegetables from a friendly rancher near Flagstaff or Winslow,
he might cook up some sourdough bread, fried peanut butter,
canned macaroni, cornmeal mush and sometimes just berries
or rattlesnake. "How cruel that gustatory delight should be so
transient," he wrote to his mother in Los Angeles.

In Arizona, he rode broncos, branded and castrated cattle,
and explored prehistoric cliff dwellings where he wrote, "The
silent centuries invade." He worked with archaeologists exca-
vating near Kayenta, Arizona. He was the only white man to
be painted by the Hopi for their ancient Antelope Dance. He
spoke Navajo, sang their songs and once, with a painted brave,
he chanted prayer songs at the bedside of a sick Indian girl. In
addition, he often risked his life unnecessarily by climbing es-
carpments and diving from a great height into a river—all to the
fear and frustration of those that knew him.

Was he beginning to have doubts about himself? "Bitter
pain is in store for me, but I shall bear it. Beauty beyond all power to convey shall be mine; death may await me; not through
cynicism and ennui will I be easy prey. And regardless of what
may befall me let me not be found to lack an understanding of
the inscrutable humor of it all."

Then, in the summer before he vanished, he wrote to a
friend from a camp in War God Springs, Navajo Mountain, Ari-

zona. "When I go, I'll leave no trace. The perfection of this place is one reason why I distrust ever returning to the cities. Here, I wander in beauty and perfection. There, one walks in the midst of ugliness and mistakes."

In the fall of 1934, his letters began to reflect a kind of futility: "I have loved the red rocks, the twisted trees, and the red sand blowing in the wind, the slow sunny clouds crossing the sky, the shafts of moonlight at night. I have really lived. I have been flirting with death, that old clown. It is enough that I am surrounded with beauty. This has been a full, rich year. I have left no strange or delightful thing undone that I wanted to do."

The last mail anyone received from Everett was posted in 1934 in late November from the Mormon settlement of Escalante, 57 miles north of Glen Canyon. Everett advised that he'd be incommunicado for a month or two. Later, when his parents hadn't heard from him, they mounted a major search which triggered national publicity—and rumors. The young vagabond was seen in Mexico. Tourists reported meeting him in Tucson. A few years later, his mother dreamt that he showed up at their back door in California, whispering, "Well, here I am."

Did he drown crossing the Colorado? Was he murdered by a "bad" Navajo? Rumors of his fate will not die. When Everett was 15 years old, he penned a poem that seems eerily prophetic when read today: "Alone I will follow the dark trail, black void on one side, and unattainable heights on the other, darkness before and behind me, darkness that pulses … and is felt."

Nemo, alas, may have gone too far down the dark trail. Whenever I hike along the Colorado River or the San Juan, I imagine that I see him and he's waving back.

Let the mystery be!

Grand Canyon Secrets

*Are the broken pieces of the tower of Babel
and the Walls of Jericho here? Should I look
for the ram's horn here? Now, this sure was
the Garden of Eden....*

- "MANY HATS" BY CARL SANDBURG

O ne never knows what might fall out of a dusty, wooden library research drawer in the old western town of Flagstaff, Arizona. When a ninety-year-old yellowed clipping appeared one day at my feet, an implausible new mystery entered my life. To this day, as if it wished someone would find it, that yellowed news story raises questions which still beg for answers. What a reminder it was, in this age of informational overkill, about how little we really know about where we came from and who we truly are. Well, at least we know all we ought to know about Grand Canyon, the natural marvel people have been studying since Teddy Roosevelt's fabled days there, early in the 20th century. Yet, it was one day in the 1990s through the smoke-filled air in a Prescott, Arizona, saloon that Dr. Robert

Euler, a retired, distinguished federal scientist, made a remark-able admission: "We really know so very little, no more than one percent of what we could and should know, and that is dis-graceful."

What he was referring to was not Mars or some disease. It was the 2,200-square-mile Grand Canyon National Park, "not a show place, a beauty spot but a revelation," British author J.B. Priestly pronounced 80 years ago—perhaps "locus dei," sug-gested author Ed Abbey.

Was Dr. Euler serious?

Despite a blizzard of theories, and Euler's robust educa-tional efforts, a factual abyss exists as deep as the very canyon itself. While nary an expert has proved beyond a reasonable doubt just how the canyon was formed, many do suspect that people have lived in it for thousands of years and concede that little is known of those years. Who were those dwellers? Where did they come from? Where did they go from there? Why did they vanish? Was it drought, religious battles, shattered trade ar-rangements?

One clue has emerged from some recent research involv-ing split-twig figurines recovered, in 1963, from a limestone cav-ern in the canyon. Revealed was a radiocarbon date of 2145 BC, plus or minus 100 years, or at least 3,600 years before Columbus reportedly discovered America. Those numbers truly stunned this pilgrim who was taught in good New England schools to be-lieve that civilized life began in North America when the Euro-peans landed at Plymouth Rock in Massachusetts around 1620.

Speaking of unanswered questions and puzzles, when I be-gan to probe some of the mysteries about the Southwest, and all the geological treasures and other things that baffle the mind, the following leaped out at me. For instance, why are so many of Grand Canyon's buttes and promontories, in the words of author John C. Van Dyke, named for "blinking little divinities of India and Egypt"? Anyone pouring over a topographical map of the canyon will indeed notice that many of the bizarre rock formations have Egyptian and East Indian names. Specifically, in the area around Ninety-Four Mile Creek and Trinity Creek, there are various rock formations with names such as Tower of Ra, Horus Temple, Osiris Temple, and Isis Temple. In the Haunted Canyon area, one finds the Cheops Pyramid, Manu Temple, and Shiva Temple.

When I launched some queries about the reasons for these ancient Egyptian and East Indian names, National Park Service spokespersons replied that one of the early explorers, Clarence Edward Dutton, simply loved Egyptian and Hindu names.

Why, then, is one entire area near these names designated by the National Park Service as a forbidden zone? No hikers are allowed without a permit in the many caves found there, and no permits are granted. Numerous Grand Canyon National Park staffers explain calmly in interviews that such a policy was necessary because of those dangerous caves. "Technically, all the caves in the canyon are dangerous and are thus restricted, off-limits," I was told by Janet Balsam, Chief of Cultural Resources at the Park.

How many caves exist?

Mysteriously, no inventory has ever been created—at least not one for the general public.

Why?

A Hopi Indian legend provides another clue. According to their oral history, passed on to me by some elders, a young man, eons ago, half Hopi and half-Anglo, wandered down a secret trail into Grand Canyon. He'd made the hike often. This time, however, the adventure would be different. It would change his life forever.

Entering a colossal cave, he told of seeing urns made of copper and gold, and a stone idol sitting cross-legged and cradling a lily in each hand. Strewn along the floor, were hundreds perhaps thousands of "cat's eyes," yellow stones, each engraved with a human head. The walls were carved and etched with the faces and bodies of short people, some wearing helmets; some were nude, some partially dressed. Also, on the walls, this young man saw painted symbols that bore no resemblance to any rock art he'd ever seen.

Excited by his discovery, he raced back up the trail to tell the elders. But instead of congratulating him, they denounced him. One uncle told him that, had he been a full-blooded Hopi, they would have had to kill him. Instead, they blinded him and made him promise never to tell anyone about his discovery. Years later, he did, after the older men had died. That's how his story survived.

Is that cave, and its contents, merely a fanciful tall tale? Or could it be that, many thousands of years ago, Grand Canyon did have visitors from Egypt and Asia? Is it possible that the standard textbook story, that humans first settled the Southwest by pouring down from Alaska about 12,000 years ago, is the truly fanciful tall tale?

One who pondered that question was the distinguished artist Maynard Dixon. After encountering a group of Indians near Grand Canyon nearly 80 years ago, he wrote in his diary: "The color, the form, the manner, the cheekbone, the sharp lip and slant of eye—surely all these are descendants from Old Asia."

Old Asia? Egypt?

Rumors flew in the 1990s that a major discovery at Grand Canyon had been covered up. Much to the dismay of park officials, nosy reporters, television crews, and foreign tourists kept asking about an immense hand-hewn cave, filled with artifacts and riches from Egypt and Asia. They'd heard that many of the walls were engraved with hieroglyphics of the prehistoric peoples of North America, revealing who they were and from whence they had come.

Try though they have, park officials have had little luck burying the story of a certain Smithsonian expedition in 1909, allegedly led by G.E. Kinkaid and Prof. S.A. Jordan. It's a hard story to put down, given the fact that I found the original interviews and details in the files of the Museum of Northern Arizona resting for so long in that dusty library file drawer. It was as if the story wished to be found.

As this newspaper account unfolded, two explorers searching for minerals were on a river trip down the Green River in Utah, then down onto the main Colorado River in Grand Canyon. The trip was going well until one day, while breaking camp on the beach, they accidentally stumbled upon what they later reported to be the oldest archaeological site in the U.S. As they later declared in a press interview, the discovery of the site helps to solve the "mystery of the prehistoric peoples of North America, their ancient arts, who they were, and from whence they came."

What those explorers claimed to have discovered was a great underground citadel featuring many passageways like the spokes of a wheel, some as long as football fields. Walking through the passageways, they came upon ancient weapons of war, sharp-edged copper instruments and hundreds of mummies stacked a dozen high.

How did they find the cave? As their story goes, while camping on the Colorado River several miles down from El Tovar Crystal Canyon, the two explorers noticed stains in the sedimentary formation on the east wall about eight feet above the river bed. There was no trail to this point, and with great difficulty, Jordan and Kinkaid climbed up to a rock shelf. Above the shelf was the mouth of the cave, which could not be seen from the river. They also found steps leading thirty yards upwards from the cave's entrance to what was the level of the river at the time the cavern was inhabited. When they saw numerous chisel marks on the wall inside the entrance, they knew they'd stumbled onto something important, maybe a treasure. They would publish their findings. And so, they did.

If their discovery struck the editors of the *Phoenix Gazette* as the wildest fancy of a fictionist, it didn't prevent them from running a detailed account on April 5, 1909. A subsequent account, with all the same details, was included in Joseph Miller's book, *Arizona Cavalcade* in 1962.

In that newspaper interview back in 1909, Kinkaid and Professor Jordan told of finding tiers of mummies in the cavern, each occupying a separate rock-hewn shelf. At the head of each, they found copper cups and pieces of broken swords. After examining some of the mummies, they determined them all to be males leading them to conclude that the room they were in may have been a warriors' burial site. In another room, perhaps the main dining hall, they found urns and water vessels marked with fine designs, signifying to them "a later stage of civilization."

Still another passage led to stone bins containing seeds of

various kinds. These bins were rounded and were composed of materials that seemed to be some kind of hard cement. They also found a gray metal, which looked like a kind of platinum.

The day was getting late so they decided to explore one more chamber before they called it quits. Entering it, they were nearly overwhelmed by a "deadly, snaky smell…our lights would not penetrate the gloom, and until stronger ones are available, we will not know what the chamber contains. Some say snakes, but others belittle the idea and think it may have contained a deadly gas or chemicals used by the ancients.

"No sounds were heard, but it smelled snaky just the same. The whole underground gives one of shaky nerves the creeps. The gloom is a weight on one's shoulders, and our flashlights and candles only made the darkness blacker. Imagination can revel in conjectures and ungodly daydreams back through the ages that elapsed till the mind reels dizzily in space."

As for reeling dizzily, the explorers decided that the cavern had so many rooms and passageways that "upwards of 50,000 people could have lived in the cave." Who were they? One sculpted idol they claimed to find was that of a Tibetan; another was engraved with the head of a Malay type.

In the 1909 *Phoenix Gazette* interview, Kinkaid told the editors that, when they arrived in Yuma, Arizona, after the discovery, he'd shipped a number of relics to the Smithsonian Institution, in Washington D.C., for evaluation. Kinkaid reported that two theories existed about the origin of the Grand Canyon mummies. One is that they came from Asia, another that the racial cradle was in the Upper Nile region; a third postulated that Egyptians originated in India. "The discoveries in Grand Canyon may throw further light on human evolution and prehistoric ages," their report concluded.

Were these relics ever sent? If they were, Smithsonian officials have said that they never received them. If they did receive
the details of the discovery, then why would such a distinguished
institution hide behind a cloud of denials? For denial has been
their strategy right up to today. I was told by David Childress, a
recognized expert in the mysteries of North and South America,
that the Smithsonian hasn't budgeted such work. "They told me
they've never found Egyptian artifacts anywhere in Arizona and
they've never been involved or ever heard of such caves. I am
not satisfied with that denial."

Arizona-based anthropologist Warren Cremer has a theory: "The Smithsonian is, no doubt, educated in the prevailing
isolationist dogma that no Europeans came to America before
Columbus in 1492, so officials there probably genuinely believe
that the finding of prehistoric Egyptian artifacts just couldn't be
true. It's time for the stonewalling to end."

"Poppycock," Grand Canyon Park Official Janet Balsam told
me. "A couple of people with a wild imagination can get away
with a lot. There is no limit to their imaginations. We regard the
tale of Egyptians in Grand Canyon as an April Fool's Joke."

However, to the Hopi today, the story is no joke and goes
beyond mere theory. One of their traditions holds that their
ancestors once lived in the underworld in Grand Canyon until
dissension arose between the good and the bad people, defined
respectively, as those with one heart, and those with two hearts.

Machetto, who was their chief, advised them that the time
had come for them to leave the underworld. But there was no
way out. The Chief then caused a tree to grow up high enough so
that it pierced the roof of the underworld. Out climbed the peo-

ple of one heart, and for years they grew corn on the banks of the Paisisvai, meaning the Red River; red, the color of the Colorado River before all the modern dams, before waters became green.

According to the legend, their elders sent a messenger to the Temple of the Sun, asking the blessings of peace, good will, and rain for the people of one heart. That messenger never returned. But today in the Hopi villages at twilight, it is said that the elders can be seen sitting on their housetops, gazing at the sun. When the Sun God returns, they believe, their ancient lands and ancient dwelling place in Grand Canyon will be returned to them.

Not with the roll of thunder drums,
but softly, soundlessly as beseems
The alchemist of color dreams,
The Sun God comes...it is a red and purple mystery.

- JOHN C. VAN DYKE

Though the news never made it into the mainstream media, groundbreaking DNA studies, first reported by *American Archeology* magazine in 1999, have determined that New World founding populations may have come from a number of regions. Molecular anthropologist Theodore Schurr and his colleagues have studied the DNA of Asian and Amerindian populations and sorted them into groups A, C, and D and postulate groups which may have arrived in the Americas as early as 30,000 years ago.

In addition, another Group B, may have been brought by a second immigration between 13,000 and 17,000 years ago, either along the Pacific coast, or overland, or both. And now here's the revelation: "The absence of the X dna grouping in Asia and Siberia and its presence among certain European populations," says Robson Bonnichsen, the Director of the Center for the Study of the First Americans at Oregon State University, suggests another migration to the Americas, besides the one in the history books—crossing the Bering Straits, then south.

It was the late Thor Heyerdahl, who spent his life trying to prove that an Atlantic crossing to South America was possible with the technology that existed in ancient times. So, in 1969, he built a ship of reeds called Ra based on an Egyptian design and launched her from the port of Safi in Morocco. The ship survived in the Atlantic for 56 days before she became dangerously leaky. A second ship reached a Caribbean island safely.

To David Childress, author of *Lost Cities of North & Central America*, the finding of the mummies all those years ago confirms oceanic contact from what is now the Mid-East, and also substantiates stories that today's tribal people didn't all cross to the Southwest by the Bering Straits. Some came by boat from the Caribbean—and into Grand Canyon.

Let the mystery be!

Miracle in Red Rock Country

In wildness is the preservation of the world.

- HENRY DAVID THOREAU

O ut in Arizona's Red Rock Country in a willowy box canyon, a coyote is pawing an ancient rock, sniffing for the oils an amphibian may have embedded there millions of years ago. High on a rocky rim overlooking this wonderland of wildness, it is said that around twilight, an old man named Kittredge finds a flat rock to sit upon and takes in the scene. As the sun disappears over the rocky rim, he reflects on the fact that the history of this place would have been much different had it not been for a phone call—and the presence of a rare bird—so many years ago. Yes, quite different, from wilderness to bulldozers, then a golf course, maybe a commercial jeep enterprise or world class resort.

Today, his canyon is being protected for the animals, and hides memories and mysteries in a sanctuary difficult to get to, one of those places time has left behind. Once there, one is truly just a guest.

New to the job as the Nature Conservancy's Arizona Director back in 1984, genial Dan Campbell was crammed into a small, stuffy, onetime dentist's office in Tucson when he received a telephone call from a man up in Sedona. Never in the world did Dan guess that the phone call might change his life and that of the Verde River and Valley, as well as its extraordinary 6,646 square miles of watershed. "Hi, I'm Bob Kittredge," the caller said in a gravelly voice, "You with the Nature Conservancy? Well, I've got a special place in a canyon near Sedona you have to see."

Campbell responded that the Conservancy did only projects of biological importance, those having to do with rivers, streams and wetlands. Undeterred, Kittredge pressed on. "Well, come up anyway. There's something interesting to see. I need your help. You see, I'm fed up with the Forest Service. They made me an offer because they want to build a campground for four-wheelers and then sell it to developers. Come up here and help me keep them out. Not only do I not want to sell it to them, I want to give it to you."

Campbell found himself in a quandary. The Conservancy had no interest in going to war with the Forest Service, and there couldn't be any rivers in his caller's canyon so the only rationale for going to Sedona, as he recalled, was that "Bob sounded like a good soul." So up into Red Rock Country he went. He met Kittredge on his land and was stunned to see a peregrine falcon nest, a sight that Arizona Game and Fish experts later said was impossible, so endangered was that crow-sized bird, capable of speeds up to 200 miles per hour. But it was the reported presence of that rare bird that opened the door for the Conservancy's involvement.

As time went by, the Conservancy accepted the gift of Kittredge's wild, remote land. Bob and his wife, Mary, would be allowed to live there if they created an endowment to cover expenses and taxes, and would take care of the special place until his death. Thus was created an island of biodiversity amidst growing commercial pressures in the region. And also a long and fruitful friendship was born between Kittredge and Campbell, who found the Sedona man to be "one of the most colorful and interesting people I've ever met."

At Bob Kittredge's death at 93 years in 2003, the Conservancy formally took charge of the 50-acre spread in a canyon in Red Rock Country and began to develop a management plan calling for limited public visitation. And therein hangs a series of mysterious tales that might strike some as too tall but, upon examination, are taller still.

Today, visitors to this remote natural paradise in Red Rock Country find themselves on a nearly impassable pot-holed red dirt road that leads into a canyon with three fingers, the longest of which unfolds back for miles. A fence line extends from stunning butte wall to butte wall in order to discourage range cattle.

One day, a geology expert among the visitors looked aghast at the multi-colored canyon walls, amazingly alive not just biologically but spiritually, as layers change in color and character by the hour. These walls revealed at least 300 million years of time in the layers called Kaibab, Toroweap, Coconino sandstone, Hermit shale and Supai deposits uplifted like a chocolate cake from sea level by indescribable powers.

As the terrain unfolded to visitors one day, a young black colt trotted up to them. Soothed by wildness, all their senses tuned, they pulled out their nature books. High above, a turkey vulture eyed them, rocking on coal-black wings as if it was philosophizing. Soon visitors became aware ahead and around them of a wonderland of shaggy-bark juniper, manzanita, oak, pinion pine, alligator juniper and ponderosa pine. From time to time, in that place, elk and pronghorn antelope appear while javelina, coyote and bear live without fear of hunters or commercial tours. A tiny spring yields 15 gallons a day, also a veritable oasis as it has been for earlier homesteaders, and the indigenous people who'd lived there a thousand years ago, or more. Now, as then, the silence there can be deafening.

In the fall, black bears wander down the last remaining undisturbed wildlife corridor from Flagstaff to fatten up on prickly pear cactus, manzanita and juniper berries. Animals can relax there, no need to be on guard. All the other canyons have undergone significant change: fewer bear in the fall, fewer birds and fewer javelinas because of constant human disturbances. Despite surrounding changes, this canyon confirms the possibility of "the geography of hope" in the words of Wallace Stegner, all because of a phone call two decades ago and the sighting of a peregrine falcon.

Where is that peregrine falcon? No one has seen it for years. It IS a rare bird.

Let the mystery be!

The Gambling Gal

It hits like a summer Monsoon. It just happens.
It is like I was sucked into a big hole, and was too
dazed to climb out. Life became unmanageable,
I became angry, distant, resentful, confused
about everything of importance in my life.
Suicide was on my mind.

- HELEN

n the evening, in the lobby near the stairs leading down into one of Arizona's smoky, raucous Indian gambling casinos, two young girls were playing pinball. Helen, grandmother of one of the girls, had given them a handful of quarters to keep them busy while she played the slots in the main casino. Once in a while, however, she'd wander over to see if the kids were hungry, or whether they might need some more change. As Helen approached them early that evening, she heard one of the young girls say to the other:

"Wouldn't it be terrible scary if your granny lost everything?

I mean the house, the car, her job? I hear that some people even go to jail."

"Don't be silly," Helen's granddaughter replied. "She's just having fun. You know how hard she works. And better stop saying such nasty things if you still want to be my friend. She can't work all the time, you know."

Years later, Helen told me that a big chunk of her secret world had fallen to pieces that same day. But what the hell, she remembered concluding at the time, she was on a winning streak that evening—and back then, winning was all.

It was scarcely a year later that Helen did find herself in the state prison near Yuma, Arizona. And, one day she called me. Despite the passage of time, I remember the phone call, and I remember how distressed I felt. Once she'd been one of my Sedona writing students, and ironically, I recalled that one class assignment had been to write about what it would be like to be in prison. Now she didn't have to make up any details.

"Can you help me, Jim?" she sobbed. "I feel as if I've been sucked into a deep hole, and there is no way out. I don't want to live any more." That was all she said. She must have dropped the prison pay phone. I could hear it banging against a wall.

At the time, I felt a pang for this woman, the first gambling addict I'd ever encountered. What had she done to deserve jail? And what could I do about it? What I did know was that, if her call was about money for a high-priced Phoenix lawyer, I couldn't hack it what with alimony payments and college tuition for my children. But I could write to her and send her books, and that I did. All I knew about her up to that point was that Helen, middle-aged and attractive, with bright blue eyes, had been working on a book, holding down a steady job, enjoying people she worked with and spending as much time as possible with her daughter and granddaughter.

But what if what she told me was wrong? What if her real life was a total mystery?

There were her stories of growing up in Maine, where she worked in the potato fields, and of receiving her early education in a one-room schoolhouse. In high school, she earned the best grades, was regarded as one of the pretty girls, and certainly was one of the shyest.

But that was then!

It was later that I learned from newspaper clippings that my old student, while living in a small village near Yuma, Arizona, and the Mexican border, did lead a mysterious, secret life.

Clothed in a white cotton bathrobe one morning, Helen was in her kitchen cheerfully making banana bread for her grandchildren, watching cartoons in the living room. Over the giggling and earsplitting clamor of the TV, she heard vehicles pulling up the gravel driveway in front of her one-story adobe bungalow. Peering out from the small kitchen window, she saw two uniformed officers walking up to her front door. She thought nothing of it; living so close to the Mexican border, there was nothing unusual about law officers looking around for illegal aliens.

Pulling the robe tighter around her slim body, she opened the front door to greet the officers, maybe offer them some coffee, only to face the first officer holding out a pair of handcuffs. "We know all about you, you're likely an addict and a felon, and you're facing time," he said firmly, clamping the cuffs around her wrists.

An addict? A felon?

Good lord, she neither smoked nor drank. Clearly, somebody had screwed up. "What about the children? I can't leave them," Helen protested. "I can't leave them alone." The officer said that a policewoman would stay with them until arrangements could be made with members of her family. "Arrangements? They are my flesh and blood. You are making a huge mistake," Helen howled at the officers through her tears.

As the little children gathered around, crying and confused, Helen raised her voice. "I have friends, you know, and I am the senior member of my family. I have a job. Mother of God."

"You need a lawyer," the officer replied. "God has nothing to do with this."

"I can't afford a lawyer," she muttered.

A few hours later, she found herself in an orange jumpsuit being escorted to her cell and being jeered at by the other women in the cell block. "Hey, look what we got here, some new white pussy, what you gone and done?" teased a woman in the next cell, "You cut your boyfriend a second one?" Laughter reverberated around the cellblock.

What on earth had happened to this seemingly proper, hardworking mother and grandmother, who could brighten up a room with a big wide smile? Simply put, like Caliban in Shakespeare's play *The Tempest*, she'd been caught out. Suddenly she was like all the other women who lead secret, mysterious lives and are eventually overwhelmed by a great compulsion to gamble, which, of all the addictions, is the most elusive of all. There are no visible signs, no slurring of words, no marks on the arms, no boozy breath. No test exists for the gambling addict, no blood tests, no X-rays. Yet, for women, this addiction hits like a tornado, furious and hypnotic, destroying marriages, demolishing financial assets and blowing away lives.

Truth be known, the destruction ends up being the same: Women who gamble only for recreation on special occasions—slot machines, blackjack, bingo, video poker—suddenly plunge in deeper as a way to "escape" from a variety of emotional problems. What once was acceptable social entertainment becomes a passion that's usually nurtured at first by a winning phase followed frequently by a traumatic event in their lives. Then, a losing phase hits them, and a period of shame and guilt is ushered in as they arrive at a fork in the road. Either they decide to continue down the path to more gambling, borrow more and more to cover their losses until desperation leads to a loss of job, or family, to cascading legal problems and even suicide, or, as Helen eventually did, they decide to seek help.

What had Helen done to deserve jail?

Why had that little girl's fear become real?

As she told me years later, she'd been caught at her job embezzling funds to cover gambling losses. At first, when her thievery was detected by an in-house auditor, her boss, whom she adored, refused to believe the accusations against her. After he examined the facts from the firm's outside auditor, however, he stepped back and refused to have anything to do with her. She'd been stealing from the company for years by kiting company checks to false companies, then cashing them.

For Helen, spending seven months in prison is a memory that will not fade. She recalled being one of six women handcuffed and chained together. A young woman in front of her asked, "Where are they taking us?" Another woman snapped. "Out back to shoot us, I hope."

Seven months were followed by seven years of parole during which time she could not vote, get a mortgage or have her
own checking account.

The week that she was released, she called to invite me to
come down to the Salt River Valley for a meal. She wanted to
thank me for the books I had sent her in prison and to share
some details of her former secret life. She thought there might
be a book in it.

Over plates of sizzling Mexican food, she shared some
details of her gambling days. "I'd stay at the machine until my
bladder nearly burst. Then, when I did leave for a moment, I'd
ask someone to watch the machine. I knew that what I was doing was stupid. I hated myself. But at the same time I loved the
scene, the people, and the excitement in those casinos. I was
alive. My brain was working. Once in a while I would put on a
wig and wear different clothes in case one of the security men
had his eye on me for always playing the same slot machine."
Helen insisted that the mess she'd created was not really about
money but about being in the ACTION, the panorama, the dra-
ma. "Before long," she told me, "I became a Zombie, who only
came to life in a casino. There I felt some kind of power and a
sense of empowerment, of being intelligent and attractive. I felt a
great independence from controlling family members. It was so
intoxicating, a good high for a while, but ultimately totally false."

She did not make a conscious decision and say, "Gee, I think
I'll become a compulsive gambler." Gambling had never inter-
ested her. She even thought it was boring, a waste of time. But

after she went to a casino during a bowling tournament and won a few jackpots on the slots, she thought, Gee. I can't lose. I could make a living doing this. I won't have to work. "So after that I got kind of hooked and started going every weekend. It was fun."

It was then that she began to lie, telling family members that she was taking college courses when she was off gambling. It all seemed so innocent. "I ignored the voice within me that kept saying, 'you're losing, stupid.' I don't know why I ignored that voice. One night I heard another lady who frequented the casino say, 'I hate this I hate this. No! I am a professional. I just keep on winning.'" It occurred to Helen that maybe she was a professional, too. But she was wrong because what she truly had become was a woman on a high for a while, a short while.

When addicts are out of prison, determined never to gamble again and intent on rebuilding a normal family life, some seek recovery and decide to pursue in-patient hospital treatment. However, that was not the path she chose. "It was up to me to decide that I had an illness and it was up to me to develop the desire to get well. In treatment, professionals take the lead in developing that desire. For some, that is the best path. But it was not for me."

She told me that her path was to attend Gamblers Anonymous meetings with other addicts at which the only ticket for attendance was to admit that gambling had them licked, that life had become unmanageable. She told me that seeking a higher power outside of herself was the answer for her. At the same time, she decided to take some community college courses and look for a job. As a felon she knew what barriers lay ahead. She ran into them during the first appointment that had been arranged by an employment agency.

The available position was to be a children's chaperone at a local Phoenix School. The interview was going well until the headmaster looked at her resume again. "I notice that uh, uh...."

"I knew what he wanted to say but couldn't and I answered, 'Yes?'"

"It says here that you are an uh, uh, uh...."

"Felon?" she answered.

With a sigh of relief, he mumbled, "Yes, but what does that mean? You don't look like a felon."

So she told him her version of the story of her compulsive gambling, that she had embezzled to support her habit but that she did not gamble anymore. His response was: "This is not the right position for you. When kids go out on their day trips, they carry lunch boxes with usually between 20 or 35 cents in them. This may be a temptation for you."

Finally, she was hired by a large corporation because the man who interviewed her believed her when she said: "If I commit another crime, it's back to prison for me. I am probably the most honest employee in the Southwest."

These days, she visits me in Sedona and leads a life she describes as marked by periods of peace and serenity. The horrors of the past sometimes visit her in discussions at Gamblers Anonymous meetings, but she now has the coping skills to work through situations instead of running or hiding. "I have learned to forgive myself for my past, but never will I forget what I did. My life has changed so much for the better that I am pretty damn sure that I'll never have to battle with myself to stop gambling again."

Soon, she was helping other women by sharing her experiences in recovery. She talked of how it began in her apartment where she met with one or two women who made the leap to the anonymous meetings for gambling addicts that had always been dominated by men.

So what did Helen find the strength to do? Eventually, she launched an all-woman's group. Via the magic of E-mail, she got in touch with women in trouble because of gambling in Australia, Great Britain and Canada. She also edits a newsletter that's mailed to women in a dozen foreign countries. In Arizona alone, there are hundreds of women in recovery, and she hopes to be busy in her role of helping women who are gambling addicts. Today, I am told by several gambling therapists that she is regarded by friends and colleagues as a hero for choosing to recover and for her leadership in helping other women to recover, living proof that compulsive gambling is not a disgrace but a diagnosable and treatable disease from which one can recover.

If there is one thing Helen knows for sure, it is that she'd be long dead had she not found her spiritual path, really dug into herself, and conducted a moral inventory, confessed personality defects, made amends to those she'd hurt and begun to reach out to others in similar straits who have yet to believe in a power greater than themselves. Without the constant urge to gamble, and the lying and cheating that accompanies it, she's now free to enjoy family and friends. People think it's a mystery that she's still alive. The mystery remains: why is it that so many addicts do fall through the cracks, causing as much damage, pain and disarray as cancer, and taking almost as many lives?

Let the mystery be!

The Lady Who Blew the Whistle

Life shrinks or expands according to one's courage.

- ANAIS NIN

For thousands of years, people have inhabited the Colorado Plateau, 130,000 square miles of startling mountains, rivers, and canyons in the Four Corners region of the southwestern United States. Descendants of those prehistoric people still inhabit this vastness, so rich in scenic wonder and cultural sites. For countless curious visitors from all over the world, fascinated by the geological, biological and biotic history of the region, one of the best places to start their education since 1928 has been the Museum of Northern Arizona. Nestled in pine groves outside of Flagstaff, Arizona, its stone buildings strike one to be as permanent a treasure as the soaring mountains looming near it. Most members believed that to be true and there was no reason to think otherwise.

Meet a gal who did think otherwise. Like that main character in Ibsen's *An Enemy of the People*, my friend Cynthia Perin challenged the institution she loved, that very museum. It was not in her background to go around stirring people to action—especially friends who were longtime members of the museum. However, she and other members sensed signs of trouble. Staffers being fired for no reason, a shortage of basic materials for classes. The deeper she dug, the more evidence she unearthed that all was not well with the museum's finances, that treacherous financial waters lay ahead, rough enough to threaten the celebrated institution's very existence. Love mixing with anger, she tried to recruit other museum members to the cause of revealing skullduggeries by the museum's then highly regarded Board of Trustees—secretly selling priceless artifacts. Few believed her facts, and most just walked away when she made her case. At that point, with little help, she went out on her own and before her crusade for ethics and honesty came to an end, both her health and her pocketbook had suffered severely.

Echoing the Ibsen plot, as soon as she began to protest under-the-table dealings by some trustees and officers, she was denounced as a trouble-making heretic, a hysterical woman. These accusations flew, not just from the mouths of most of the trustees of that great museum (a celebrated repository of tribal artifacts), but from members of her own family, including a cousin who called her a "malicious liar."

Still others compared her to the manipulating Lily Bart, the notorious heroine in Edith Wharton's "House of Mirth." Friends she'd known for years left the room when she walked in, while others ridiculed her in letters to the local newspapers.

To this day, she remains saddened that many of her friends were content to hide in their caves of denial. As time went by, she was no longer all alone; others were writing letters of complaint about the financial troubles ahead for the museum and attempted to enlighten other museum members. Throughout, however, it was Cynthia who had the greatest passion. Why was she leading the battle? "There was a crocodile in the bathtub," she told me later. To many trustees, highly paid staffers and others, she was the crocodile.

Her lonely campaign began in the year 2001 and was to last three years. By the time the curtain came down, and various scoundrels had been sent packing, it was clear to the renegade trustees of the Museum of Northern Arizona that they had never had to deal with such a cyclone of a woman before. Then again, not many museum trustees had ever woven such a web of lies or fooled so many loyal members for so long.

What appeared at first to be a minor staffing adjustment turned out to be the trigger which launched her crusade. A research librarian at the museum had been fired for no apparent reason—and Cynthia had been funding his position. Furious, she bombarded the trustees with mail, at least 124 letters in all in which she protested the firing, allegedly for poor performance. "What a bald-faced lie," she wrote to the trustees. "It is true, after all, that there is no honor among thieves. I find the actions of the Museum's trustees to be extremely disgraceful, unprofessional and unethical."

Harsh words, but she knew she'd been lied to by the director. It was a moment she'd never forget. "My insides turned into a combo of mush and rage," she recalled later. When she'd asked him why the librarian was fired, she'd been told that he wouldn't do what he was told to do, and there were no longer the funds to pay him.

"That's not true, and you know it," Cynthia jumped in. "I want to know why."

"I can't tell you," the director replied.

"You don't have enough money to pay him? That just couldn't be since I pay most of his salary."

"There's nothing we can do."

"Look, I'll give you more money to pay his salary."

"That's not necessary. We have decided."

At that, Cynthia stomped out, realizing that she'd found the fox in the proverbial chicken coop. What she didn't know was that, once she was out of hearing distance, the director gloated to his secretary, "Well, Cynthia took that well enough. Guess we'll have no trouble from her." Yet, as the weeks wore on, various museum topsiders discovered they had misjudged her. Almost overnight, she had become a relentless investigator. To begin with, she'd decided that the two well paid museum officials she'd been dealing with were "two little boys dressed up in men's clothing who refused to take responsibilities for their own actions." She told friends that, when she had the chance, she was going to "nail their asses to the cross." That was rough talk, brimming with unlady-like curse words. To put it mildly, this did not make her many new friends; many still believed that the museum was in fine financial shape. Wasn't that what the trustees were telling them?

Undeterred, she dug up some clues as to why the bright, young librarian was fired. Was it because he knew too much? Had he seen something he shouldn't have? Backward raced her mind, until she recalled a brief but odd moment in the museum's research wing a year earlier. By tradition, that area was closed to visitors, so who was that mysterious couple seen by the librarian, preparing to enter the vault where the museum's archives and rarest of special collections were stored—priceless paintings by Maynard Dixon; extraordinary Navajo weavings, so valuable that their worth could not be determined; the Barry Goldwater photos, and other priceless documents.

Already suspicious of the seditious actions at the museum, she discovered that its leaders were on the verge of doing the unthinkable: Selling the rarest pieces in the permanent collection to cover operating expenses—which would violate a host of rules and regulations, not to mention federal tax laws. Virtually overnight, this well bred, gently raised horsewoman, longtime museum donor and volunteer, had transformed herself into an activist, a combination of The Shadow, Sherlock Holmes, and Mother Jones.

Late one night in the shower, Cynthia suddenly grasped the true facts. Were those out-of-town people dealers, ready to take away the museum's principal assets? Because her uncle had once been director of the museum, she knew something about legal issues in that esoteric world: No museum is allowed to sell its own collection, its very endowment, unless the sale is intended to enhance that collection or to build another building. Under no circumstance may valued collections be sold to pay debts. Should that occur, the museum would violate the ethical standards of the American Association of Museums and thus lose hard-earned accreditation.

Slowly, the truth emerged. Some board trustees had a special notebook displaying the prized items for sale, totaling close to one million dollars. Time and again, when she asked the museum leaders to admit what they were up to and to level with her, herself a longtime contributor, she was told by a trustee to "calm down." One of her own brothers, a trustee, refused to speak to her.

Relentlessly, Cynthia pestered the museum staff for the paperwork that would document the forthcoming sale. She learned that a dealer from New Mexico was to receieve $100,000 to handle the sale of the museum's precious artifacts. "It was disgraceful," Cynthia recalled to me later. "Not one trustee took a stand against the sale. They looked the other way. They had to have approved it."

In those troubled times, Cynthia made a habit of walking the museum grounds in hopes of bumping into staff people she'd known for years; maybe they'd lead her to more damning evidence. One day, she went to the museum's administrative office and asked to see the tax forms of the senior staff. She knew that many of them were highly paid, but she wanted to see if they'd given themselves large raises recently. Come back tomorrow, she was told. On the way to her vehicle, she met the man in charge of the museum's grounds, someone she'd known for years. "Cynthia, please don't be mad at me, but I have orders to throw you off the grounds. I'm sorry, but the orders come straight from the trustees. If you don't leave, I will lose my job." She agreed to leave, assuring a friend later that day "Now I'm really going to get those [expletives deleted]."

The more she dug, the more she found; yet the more the mystery deepened. Despite mounting debt, museum trustees and senior staff inexplicably refused to take the steps traditionally used by nonprofit organizations to raise funds to avoid financial calamity. Now, as she'd feared, calamity was headed at them like a runaway bus. "They never fulfilled their obligations as trustees," Cynthia exclaimed. Most of all, once the sales went through, no one would tell her where the money went from the sale.

Soon, under fire for other reasons, such as his inability to raise funds, the museum's recently hired director departed for good, and a series of acting presidents took over. At the same time, some of the trustees were getting nervous. They were fearful that word would leak about their unethical activities. Ironically, it was at that moment that the trustees took the step that ultimately proved to be their undoing. The famed Geology Department was ordered closed right before the opening of a big show.

How could that be? Cynthia knew that the Geology Chair was funded by outside benefactors in the form of an endowment. Letters, phone calls and personal meetings followed, but no one would give her a straight answer about all the financial mischief. Her trustee brother told her to back off, that no museum board ever resigned due to the pressure of one person. Turns out he hadn't heard of the Badgers.

Once a week, this devoted group of museum members— retired teachers, business people, hikers, scientists—met in an auto dealer's conference room, far from any of the places in town where they might be seen. Day by day, they walked the streets of Flagstaff, Tucson, Phoenix, Prescott, seeking citizens to sign petitions to throw out the current trustees. To do this, they needed signatures of 10 percent of the membership, or 350 names. Cynthia secured the services of a lawyer. His specialty was the nonprofit organization. Regularly, the attorney met with the group and told them what they could and could not do. In common, their goal was to get rid of the malefactors in charge of the museum, retrieve the lost art and find out where the money from the sale of artifacts had gone.

Even now the identity of each of the Badgers remains unknown, other than the fact that they were men and women of all ages and sizes who lined up beside Cynthia and carried out various missions. Then came the breakthrough that shocked members and media alike. Cynthia remembered the name of the man years ago who was the principal donor to the geology program. Cynthia recalls the first conversation via a telephone between her and Malcolm McKenna, a crusty, no-nonsense character in Colorado.

"So you're the woman with a brother on the museum board. Well, I am sorry for you."

"I'm sorry for me, too."

"Well, you're one strong person. I'd like to get to know you."

Together, they hatched a plan to bring down the trustees for their unethical actions. At the next yearly meeting in June 2003, McKenna agreed to attend and wear a disguise to avoid being spotted by older trustees. Her assignment was to meet him before the meeting near a certain tree they both knew on the museum grounds. At the appointed hour, Cynthia spotted an elegant gentleman sporting a head of white hair and wearing a bright blue shirt.

"Are you Mr. Badger?"

"Ah yes," he replied, and turning, walked into a large room of raucous men and women who were often booing the museum's trustees, seated at the front of the room. By design, the Badgers were scattered here and there around the meeting room. Tension rose in the air as one of the Badgers put a question to the trustees: Did any of them talk to the donors of the geology program before it was shut down? Did any one of them talk to Malcolm McKenna? "Yes" came the answer, "many times."

At that point, one of the Badgers pushed through the crowd

to give a mike to McKenna, who was standing against the wall in the back of the room. Said he to the entire assembly, "I am McKenna. I find it interesting that you have spoken to me many times as a donor of the geology program because, you see, it is not true. I had one call. It was about something else."

A roar went up in the room. Respectable people stomped their feet on the floor and booed. The meeting was over. Because of that admittance and the fact that donors were pulling back, and the Badgers' petition campaign was working, the entire board of trustees resigned on July 26, 2003.

These days, years after the old board resigned, calmer hours prevail at the Museum of Northern Arizona. It did lose its accreditation for quite a while, but that has been restored. A new board of trustees is now in place, and so is an acclaimed new director. Funds are being raised. A wonderful new award-winning million-dollar building, the Easton Collections Center, has been erected, and has won many awards, one as greenest building in Arizona, if not the greenest in the nation.

Nevertheless, mysteries remain.

What happened to the art that was sold?

What happened to the money from the sale of the artifacts?

How could the board of trustees ever have thought they could get away with it?

"It was criminal," asserts Bill Breed, a well respected scientist with years of ties with the museum. "If it hadn't been for Cynthia...."

"She's a brave kid," remembered her old riding pal, 95-year-old Mary Kittredge. "She took a lot for a good cause. She was no enemy of the people, she was their friend. "

Ironically, even today some people look the other way

when she enters a room, to them a prophet with little honor in her own town. Sums up Cynthia, "People figured that because I'm a woman, they could control me, that I couldn't chase the foxes from the hen house. They were as wrong as two left shoes."

Curiously, the world will never know all the details of the settlement agreement between the Santa Fe dealer and the museum for they are sealed forever by court order.

What if Cynthia hadn't accepted the challenge? "The museum has come through probably the most turbulent time in its history. In the tradition of its founders, Dr. Harold Colton and Mary Ferrell Colton, MNA stands ready to welcome, to delight, and to teach," states author, museum stalwart Bennie Blake. "Now, and since 1928, its heavy wooden doors swing wide for those who still come to explore its treasures."

Without Cynthia those doors would have been closed forever. Why was it that so many loyal museum supporters looked the other way?

Let the mystery be!

The Dying River

O flowing river feed the well
Before you leave, and say "farewell."
You've gone away, the well is dry.
I often ask and wonder why.

- AMERA ANDERSEN

"I t's a mystery to me why most folks don't realize what's happening," grumbled supervisor Chip Davis as he stomped around his Yavapai County office not far from the Verde River in central Arizona. In his hands was a newspaper flashing the headline "River Runs Dry." The story reported that a stretch of the San Pedro River, which had flowed for centuries southeast of Phoenix, had gone dry. But Davis was not referring to the San Pedro. He was talking about the Verde River, Arizona's only indigenous river, the source of 30 percent of Greater Phoenix's water supply, and upon which 3.5 million citizens depend.

Davis's concern is that the Verde River could go the way of the San Pedro, for the same reasons—uncontrolled groundwater pumping, runaway growth, all of which would decimate extraordinary wildlife, from otters and beaver, to cougars, bald eagles and native fish.

Developers label Davis a trouble-making environmentalist, needlessly fearful that the ancient river is being asked to give more than it has to give. His friends point out that, in fact, he is a fourth generation Republican cut in the mold of Teddy Roosevelt, that, in fact, he belongs instead in the hallowed tradition established by the now-extinct moderate Republicans responsible for the passage of environmental laws during the Nixon Administration. More to the point, he's faced with the fact that few believe his warnings about the possibility that the river may die. It is as if he'd been cursed, like Cassandra from Greek Mythology, so that nearly no one believes his predictions.

While most politicians continue to ignore him, warning signs are everywhere. Hydrologists in Yavapai County, nearly as large as New Jersey, report that wells and a large spring have gone dry. Yet that's the least of it. What really can interrupt Davis's sleep are the City of Prescott's plans to import water from a well field near the headwaters of the Verde River. Prescott officials deny that pulling water, 14,000 acre feet annually, from the aquifer threatens the Verde. (As a rule of thumb in U.S. water management, one acre-foot is taken to be the planned water usage of a suburban family household, annually.)

Davis disagrees. "It strikes me as hazardous to export that much water when the recharge rate is quite a bit less than that. We don't know what the impact will be, but it will be real. Who would have thought ten years ago that one well field could have the effect of drying up a river fifteen miles away?"

Another matter worrying him is that Flagstaff and Williams are in the process of sinking 3000 foot wells. Will they be drilling into the aquifer that feeds the Verde?

The other "elephant in the living room," says Davis, "is that future developments could dwarf the impacts of the forthcoming Prescott project. There are hundreds of thousands of acres out there, private and state-owned, yet the county is prohibited by state law from determining water usage in housing and commercial developments. I have zero ability."

Zero ability? Believe it or not, Davis lacks the power to protect the Verde in a county which grew by 55.5 percent from 1990 to 2000: "Tools, I have no tools. By state law, counties are forbidden to consider water issues when matters of zoning change and land use come before them. We can't deny a project because we think there is no water. We cannot even mention the word."

Because of a state legislature mired in the Middle Ages, politics has trumped science. Most politicians have turned a blind eye to the scientific facts. As Davis tells visitors, few legislators are from rural areas. Therefore, due to the size of Tucson and Phoenix, most of the legislation is determined by elected officials from urban areas. But there's an even larger problem! Although some rural counties are facing explosive growth and challenging water issues, most other rural counties, such as Apache, Navajo, Gila, Cochise, Greenlee are not booming. "The legislators from those counties would do anything to grow," says Davis, "so they fight any legislation that would give counties the power to regulate water use."

Friends and supporters see Davis as a poorly armed lawman with thieves and vultures at his back. Nonetheless, he remains resolute. "As responsible custodians, you'd think we'd have a statewide goal of building a healthy and sustainable Arizona, instead of one of grab-all-you-can as quick as you can because the ship will soon sink."

In this land of beauty, pioneers and tribes, where John Wayne and Jimmy Stewart made Westerns, why then are so many citizens sleep-walking into the future? Sums up Arizona writer/historian Steve Ayers, who can't put his finger on that mystery, either, "As long as the Verde flows, we are demonstrating our love for what we were given—as well as love for one another. If the Verde were to disappear, we would reveal that our only true love was for ourselves."

Years ago, Margaret Mead proclaimed that society should "never doubt that the work of a small group of thoughtful committed citizens can change the world. Indeed it is the only thing that has."

Where are these thoughtful, committed citizens?

Let the mystery be!

Near Death of the Winemaker

*Medicine is a collection of uncertain prescriptions
the result of which, taken collectively, are more
fatal than useful to mankind.*

- Napolean Bonaparte

O n any given day, Arizona winemaker Eric Glomski will tell visitors about how the Romans raised grapes in eastern Turkey 8,000 years ago; and how the first wines were made from dates and then from grapes, which of course, were red and became symbolic for their connection to blood. However, it was not the Romans, but rather the Greeks, who believed that wine could be big business someday, so they began exporting the best wines. Of late, big business in the shape of a worldwide wine boom has reached the deserts of the Southwest, and also onto some onetime Indian land in central Arizona, the state where Glomski is the acknowledged pacesetter. Visitors to his vineyard near a town most maps overlook are challenged by this mystery: how do grapes such as Syrah and Grenache survive on such rugged, high-altitude land?

By any measure, Glomski is familiar with the mysteries, the glories and the frustrations inherent in the world of vineyards. There's the weather to worry about, condition of the soils, and insects and viruses that threaten the grapes. But when you cannot breathe or smell, then dealing with daily challenges is equivalent to trying to hold the wind back with a net. Such was Glomski's predicament as he readied his crew to harvest Syrah grapes in his vineyard in Arizona's Verde Valley on one summer day early in the new century.

In all of his 38 years in the Midwest, California and in the Southwest, never had he experienced allergies. Athletic and dedicated to leading a healthy life, he'd never needed to go to a physician, and never wanted to. He knew the statistics about medical errors, big numbers like 100,000 deaths a year—more than annual deaths from highway accidents and breast cancer; apart from that concern, he firmly believed that, should he ever become ill, the body is able to heal itself in time.

But not this time around.

Day by day, his head was becoming ever more stuffed, his nostrils more blocked. At that point, he concluded that he had no choice but to break one of his rules and visit the local emergency room. "Sinus infection," said the young physician. "Here, take these antibiotics."

And so Eric did, but nothing changed. Two weeks later, he returned to the emergency room anxious to try something else. This time, he was examined by a different physician. "Well if that antibiotic doesn't work, try this one," the second physician declared and handed him a handful of different pills. Then, Eric began to be bothered because he felt that he was violating one of his fundamental principals—never give away his power to doctors who seemed to be engaged in an elaborate match of medical guesswork. "This must stop," he told a friend.

True, he knew that antibiotics were regarded as silver bullets for healing. But what if the doctors were wrong? Maybe he had a viral condition, or some sort of food allergy. He had to find a way back to health—and soon. He was becoming short of breath and losing his sense of smell, and he knew that his vineyard staff needed his knowledge and his presence. He had to find out what was triggering this excruciating reaction. Was it sulfites in wine?

Despite feeling lousy, there was work to be done, and he had to help do it. There was a load of grapes to pick in Paso Robles, California, to bring back for processing in Arizona. With one of his staffers, he drove over in a truck and began to load grapes. Maybe that would make him feel better. At the end of the day, however, he was feeling worse. During dinner with friends at their vineyard, he felt really ill and went to a back room to be alone, to sit on the toilet and to grapple with cold sweats. He had to get home, but there was still work to be done. "God, how I wanted my own bed," he told a friend later. "I wished for my own toilet, because I had the worst case of the shits in my life. I wondered whether I'd ever get out of this. My head was spinning and I was totally dehydrated."

On the eight-hour drive back to Arizona, Eric stretched out in the back of the truck and had to stop every half hour. Then there was a new development. He was still experiencing almost continuous bowel movements, but this time nothing was coming out. "I felt as if someone had stuck a knife in my gut and was twisting it." Chugging Pepto-Bismol helped but by the time they got to Barstow, Eric pleaded to be dropped off at a hospital.

"No," said Cory, the driver, "I'm taking you home."

Back in Arizona, he tried to help the staff unload five tons of grapes, but all of a sudden he was having difficulty walking. Something was happening with the nerves in his lower back and spasms of electric pain were surging through his body. Rushing to a bathroom, he found himself passing blood, lots of it.

That was too much for his wife, Gayle, who drove him at top speed to the nearest emergency room. Eric remembers little of that visit except the constant vomiting and shitting, but nothing was coming out. The world around him had become fuzzy and blurry.

Hooking up an IV, the nurse decided that Eric needed a painkiller. As the nurse was tending to him, Gayle became queasy and came close to fainting. Soon, help arrived to put her on a stretcher in her husband's room. Whatever the brand of painkiller was, it hit him hard. Although the pain in his body began to subside, he felt that he was losing the ability to discern what was happening and to make decisions. Had his wife not been there that day to ask questions, to inform the physicians about her husband's lifestyle, eating and drinking habits, Eric believes that the hours spent in the hospital would have been far worse.

As it was, he was given many tests, including a CT-scan. Perhaps, he had a case of diverticulitis, an inflammation in the colon. This results in infected tissue surrounding the colon. Treatment? More antibiotics? It was then that a medical staffer walked into Eric's room to announce that blood had been found in his stool. Well, Eric thought to himself, what a bright intern! Didn't he know that already? Isn't that why he'd come to the emergency room in the first place?

What to do?

Suddenly, his sinus condition was forgotten because being prescribed now were more painkillers and a different kind of antibiotic. By now, Gayle had figured that he'd more than met their $5,000 insurance deductible. She was correct. Hospital charges for four hours soared well beyond that amount.

Eric's quandary was unmistakable: How could he have any faith in the medical profession when not one doctor that he'd encountered had a clue as to what ailed him? And yet, where else and to whom could he turn? Whatever, he decided, and so he took the latest in the new pills, powerful pills that tasted like copper pennies, and also caused sharp pains in his neck muscles.

Days became weeks. He tried to work and eat less because, whenever he ate anything, the pain deep in his gut became worse. Around the clock, he was still passing blood and had begun to lose weight. By the first week he'd lost ten pounds.

What next? Eric had a visit with another physician, a woman recommended to him by friends. A blood test revealed that Eric's white cell count was far too high. She had no clear guidance for him, but she gave him more pills.

Amidst it all, Eric began to read up on various bowel diseases. The thing to do, he decided, was to get an appointment with the best gastroenterologist within 200 miles from his home in Page Springs, Arizona.

Bad idea!

No appointments for six weeks, he was told. "People are dying and you are not dying yet," one staffer in a medical office in Phoenix told him, exhibiting all the charm of a puff adder.

By now, Eric concluded that he must be allergic to some kind of food. So he went on a rice diet, led by rice protein shakes, gallons of papaya juice, and all kinds of vitamins. Maybe that might help. It didn't. He'd lost 25 pounds in two weeks. Between them, he and his wife phoned all the gastrointestinal physicians they could find listed in the phonebook to determine whether there might be cancellations. No dice.

When the word was getting around that he wasn't well, many members of the local New Age community that loved him and his wine showed up with an array of miracle cures, herbs and crystals, aura detectors and various potions. He thanked them all, but their efforts came to naught.

Meantime, his absences were causing troubles at his vineyard. His normal work week lasted for 80 hours. But he couldn't do that anymore because of the pain in his gut and because he needed to be close to a toilet. Whenever he could, he'd show up to work for a few hours. However, the visits caused stress among the staff because many had not waited for him and had done the necessary decision-making. Meantime, he never stopped looked for solutions, so he turned to his brother.

Eric's brother, a PhD in immunology, works in Chicago. When he saw Eric he was shocked, "You look like a concentration camp survivor, an AIDS patient. We must keep looking for answers, maybe Crohn's disease or celiac disease, or the worst case, colon cancer."

It was right about then, two months from the day that he became ill, that he found some clues as to what was ruining his life. He learned from documents that he had gathered from a conference on bowel disease that people in third world countries experience such bowel diseases far less than those in western countries.

Why?

Because people in western countries use so many antibiotics, they have destroyed the colon's ecological balance. This was cutting edge research, he decided, and he felt that he was a guinea pig. Yet the mystery of how he was struck by it remained as elusive as sheet lightning in summertime. Though he felt he'd diagnosed himself accurately, no physician had yet to do so. So, on that level, the mystery of what ailed him remained.

One thing for certain, he was really scared. He was shitting blood as if it was coming from some unseen world. He regarded it as a metaphor for our modern approach to living. At that point, he gave up searching for cures and went to his portable computer. In short order, he e-mailed the following message to friends, politicians, winemakers, and everyone whose paths he'd crossed and who'd crossed his. The message: "Do you know any gastroenterologists who can help me? I have lost 30 pounds in eight weeks."

Shortly thereafter he received a response from an old friend in New Zealand, a movie director and a onetime winemaker. Yes, he knew of a physician in southern Arizona whose specialty was the human digestive system. His friend wrote, "And they talk about it the way we talk about wine. They look at the body as a whole and have an inflammatory bowel special unit."

A few days later, thanks to a call from Eric's old friend, the new group welcomed Eric, tested him from every conceivable angle, along with his blood. On the second day, he was told that he was suffering from malnutrition. No wonder, since he hadn't eaten any solids for six weeks. So he was offered a chicken salad sandwich. He was so hungry that he could have eaten the paper it was wrapped in and devoured that sandwich. His recovery had begun.

The greatest thing, he told me later, was that his body had

become a river and the doctors were pulling out all the trash in his body all the way back to its watershed.

Soon, the verdict was in: His body was being wracked by a massive infection characterized by his immune system attacking the inside walls of his guts.

The cause: Colitis caused by antibiotics.

From the start, he'd been wrongly diagnosed.

Why couldn't the physicians see it? What pills had he taken? Might it ever happen to him again?

Let the mystery be!

Chacho Canyon: Myth & Mystery

*Such silence and stillness and repose—
immortal repose. That village sat looking
down into the canyon with the calmness of
eternity...I had come upon the city of some
extinct civilization, hidden away in this
inaccessible mesa for centuries...guarded
by the cliffs and the river and the desert.*

- WILLA CATHER, FROM *THE PROFESSOR'S HOUSE*

round King Arthur's time in western England, people known today as the Anasazi were growing corn in a remote canyon known as Chaco in the San Juan basin in northwest New Mexico. While English people were struggling in the Dark Ages, farmers in that canyon went from living in pit houses to building pueblos featuring solar heating and cooling in 13 large villages, utilizing hundreds of thousands of logs hauled from an unknown distance. Perhaps those people's greatest feat was building Pueblo Bonito, five stories high, covering three acres, and including some 800 rooms. They also built a road system, designed to reflect the very heavens themselves. Recounts Chaco expert Douglas Preston, "The ancient Chaco road system was probably the greatest feat of engineering left to us by any prehistoric civilization. It's a visible expression of a culture that once encompassed some 75,000 square miles of the American Southwest."

As a young, listless teenager in the 1950s, I visited Chaco with my mother, the artist Lucile Brokaw, a Long Islander fascinated by so-called primitive peoples because they were so sophisticated. What was all the fuss, I remember wondering, a pile of rocks here and there, fierce dusty wind blowing hard, nothing to see. Then came some rain, making a whispering sound, like voices coming from somewhere, but where? What happened to all the people, I asked my mother. She thought a while and said, "It was as if people you knew left their house with only the clothes on their back, never, never to return again—but their spirits are here." Baloney I thought. No, it is not.

Sometime around 1300 A.D. the spectacular Chaco culture quietly collapsed, roads were closed, buildings sealed and the people departed for destinations only speculated about. Thereby hangs a mystery that has attracted scientists, film-makers, members of other tribes to try to unravel. No one knows for sure. In fact the more the research, the more questions arise seeking answers. Was it drought, famine, enemy raiders? Was it disease? Sudden climatic change? Overpopulation? Environmental damage such as deforestation? Terrorism? Whatever the reasons, a curtain fell on their golden age and the people departed, in some cases leaving pet birds behind to die on their roosts, bequeathing a ghost world for future explorers to discover. People visit the ruins today in large numbers under the aegis of the National Park Service. Opines one visitor, Roga Hudson, who has photographed tribal ruins all across the Southwest, "No prehistoric site even comes close to Chaco. The level of political integration and architecture is unrivaled in prehistoric times. Being there is like having a glimpse of a distant, mysterious world. But something very serious shook up their culture." When acclaimed New Mexico-based poet V. B. Price first visited Chaco in 1960, he recalls that it made little or no impression on him. Then inspirations and tragedies broke over him, his friends and others. "For me," he has written, "it meant poverty, depression, divorce, estrangement from beloved children, political journalism, protest and poetry." He thinks that it was a decade later when he was hiking with an old friend and his brother-in-law, and felt for the first time, "the Canyon's directness, its harsh clarity, smoothed the matrix of our confusions." Price, now a distinguished poet, author, teacher, remembers that day when he felt himself change, literally from one step to the next. "I felt my whole self become immediately aware of my whole environment."

The canyon is the center of a Self
Weightless as the silence of the rock,
A silence is felt
Pretending you're not there,
Sitting still with stones to be weathered by the day
Forgetting who you are

Lost like friends, dead sins,
Like breath
That rock time won't contain,
A stone eye opened
As eddies of birds blow past
Worlds within worlds…the silent breathing
Of the God of Gods whose name nobody knows.

Unlike Price who visits Chaco fairly often, Bennie Blake editor/explorer of Sedona's Verde Valley—and the Southwest—has explored the canyon rarely, yet every moment spent wandering there is emblazoned into her consciousness.

To friends she tells of a camping trip to Chaco, led by renowned anthropologist David Wilcox of the Museum of Northern Arizona. From her tent on the first morning she heard pans rattling and Wilcox announcing that coffee was ready. Said he, "The temperature is 10 degrees." Exposing her bare skin to 10 degrees and sliding into jeans and shirt, Blake feels she learned first hand about Chaco's extremes of weather and temperature and how it must have felt for Chacoans on a cold day in winter. After days of hiking and learning she became pensive and silent, wondering whatever caused such a fantastic civilization to vanish. Why did they seal up the buildings? Why did they never again build such structures? Somewhere in the walls she studied was the story of twelve generations of people, their intelligence, their muscle power, and the unique ability of the human to adapt. Back home in Arizona, after a welcome hot shower she went to bed. But before sleep came she recalls, "I struggled with my own sorrow at what the Chacoans had won and then lost and with my own efforts to force the unknown to yield its secrets."

No one knows what brought down the economic, ritual and social system that spread out over an estimated one hundred thousand square miles, except that something went terribly, horribly wrong.

The first to tell the tale was an hombre by the name of Christy Turner, Ph.D., author of *Man Corn* who told me flat out one horrendously hot day outside of Phoenix that the "The land of the Anasazi was not a pleasant place to be, after all. It was just as violent as any place else in the world. Mean and unhappy."

What? New Age groupies from all over the world have made much of the Anasazi culture, believing it to have been deeply spiritual, possibly connected to more advanced extraterrestrial civilizations. But wait! What if that peaceful image is wrong, very wrong? Few even dared raise such a bold question over the years for fear of discouraging tourism and tainting the image of the Nobel Savage. When they did, blank stares, angry letters and cancelled meetings were the questioners' reward.

One of the very few is the aforementioned Christy G. Turner, Arizona State University regents' professor of anthropology. Because of a series of coincidental events, the mainstream panjandrums of southwestern archaeology and anthropology can no longer ignore him. The reason is the publication of *Man Corn* by Turner and his late wife, Jacqueline. After years of rumors, it is the first detailed account of cannibalism and violence on a regional scale in the prehistoric American Southwest, especially in the Chaco Canyon area.

The title of the book comes from the Aztec word tlacatlaolli, a "sacred meal of sacrificed human meat, cooked with corn." Turner's conclusions have taken southwestern archaeology in a new direction, and it will take a long time for the dust to settle.

Old paradigms have been upset. Maybe the Anasazi were people like us, with a dark side.

Until *Man Corn,* many scientists could safely respond to the charge of cannibalism in the Four Corners region by telling reporters and others that such brutal butchery never happened. In Turner's educated opinion, however, cannibalism was practiced for almost four centuries, starting around AD 900. It was most common, especially among people living in Chaco Canyon and in or near outlying Chacoan great houses, increasing dramatically shortly before the Anasazi abandoned their sacred pueblos.

For Turner and his late wife, this assertion took a long time to construct. Years of research were required under various auspices, such as The Museum of Northern Arizona at Flagstaff, and the National Geographic Society, before Turner felt he was on sufficiently firm ground to challenge the prevailing way of thinking about the Anasazi.

Explained Turner to me in an interview: "Like others in the field, we had to work our way through the conventional wisdom that the people who created the beautiful pottery and architecture could not possibly have done these things. I mean the ruins are terribly romantic. It is beautiful country, a fantasy world and that is a great influence on lots of archaeologists. Down through the years, countless people visited the ruins. They came away with everything but the truth."

The truth is that at 76 Anasazi sites Turner confirms violence or cannibalism occurred—eleven in Arizona, the rest in Utah, Colorado and New Mexico. Amazingly, the first site, discovered by Walter Hough in May 1901 on a large butte east-southeast of Holbrook, Arizona, dated to the period A.D. 1200-

1300. Somehow, his discovery never made it into the textbooks. However, the following description did. Within a year after the excavation, Hough wrote in *Harper's Monthly* magazine:

> In the cemetery, among other orderly burials, was uncovered a heap of broken bones belonging to three individuals. It was evident that the shattered bones had been clean when they were placed in the ground, and some fragments showed scorching by fire. The marks of the implements used in cracking the bones were still traceable. Without doubt this ossuary is the record of a cannibal feast, and its discovery is interesting to science as being the first material proof of cannibalism among our North American Indians.

Turner, pointing out that many famous scientists suspected cannibalism down through the years—Fewkes, Hodge, Pepper, the Weatherills, the Listers, Pilles, White, Danson and many others—presents *Man Corn* as a tribute to them. "The vast majority saw it correctly, but their work was never acknowledged in the profession's mainstream because it flew in the face of conventional wisdom."

His inference of cannibalism raises myriad questions. First, how can scientists distinguish between violence and cannibalism? Explained Turner in the interview: "It comes directly from bone evidence. Bone damage is able to be classified, inventoried, identified and pigeonholed. It turns out that in factoring out different kinds of damage, cannibalism far exceeds anything that we can refer to as violence.

"That is because the key component in violence is simply

violent death, torture, mutilation. It stops there. There is none of this breaking up of the people; whole skeletons reduced to little tiny pieces. We can make a powerful inference that all those little pieces have been processed for cooking. In cases of violence, they didn't go to the next step of sitting down and peeling the people, defleshing them, breaking the bones open for marrow and showing us every sign of cooking—heads roasted, bodies boiled, bones pot-polished."

Across the Southwest, voices have risen in angry protest against Turner's thesis. "He has not proven a thing," charges Kurt Dongoske, Tribal Archaeologist of the Hopi Tribe. "What he has demonstrated is that people were hacked apart, their bones dismembered. He presents no evidence of human ingestion. He's way out on a limb. There are thousands of Anasazi sites and his sample covered just 77. Cannibalism was not part of the tradition. That was what happened in Mexico."

A scientist who thinks *Man Corn* should be taken seriously is David R. Wilcox, Senior Research Archaeologist at the Museum of Northern Arizona and sometime colleague of Turner's through the years. As he explained in his small office overflowing with books, coffee cups and telephone messages in the museum's research wing, "Turner presents a very reasonable scientific argument for cannibalism…but to say that all Anasazis were cannibals is not the correct inference. It is a vast generalization. It is not as though everybody did it, even if he is right.

"But that there were individuals at certain times and places that for reasons still controversial, may have conducted massacres of multiple people, then butchered and cooked and quite possibly ate them, is very difficult to deny. As for his theories as why they did it, we don't know."

The word "cannibal," Turner writes, comes from the Carib Indian tribal name, derived from Spanish, referring to a person who eats human flesh. Despite the fact that the moral is everywhere the same: eating someone is disruptive, inconsiderate, evil, "cannibalism is bad, and bad people are cannibals," Turner provides details of the practice going back thousands of years as reported in worldwide folklore, oral traditions, sacred writings, anthropological narratives, war stories, urban police records, and tales of lost wanderers about cannibal peoples and cannibal events. 'Truth to tell," declares Turner, "cannibalism has occurred everywhere at one time or another."

But why?

Turner's reasons for the occurrence of cannibalism vary from place to place around the world. They range from starvation cannibalism in the Arctic to cannibalism as a ritual element in social control in Mesoamerica; as an institutionalized way of showing love and respect for the dead in China; as a way for obtaining the power and strength of a sacrificial victim in Brazil and finally, cannibalism associated with social pathology the world over. As to the cannibalism at Anasazi sites, Turner favors a combination of three reasons: ritual human sacrifice, social control and abnormal, criminal behavior.

Another big question was this: Who were the cannibals in the Southwest and where did they come from? In *Man Corn* Turner concedes that, after many attempts to unlock that mystery, "There is no way at this time to determine who did the eating or who was eaten—friends, relatives, slaves, strangers." He reached that conclusion after searching for similar sites in California, in the Rocky Mountains, on the Great Plains and amongst Anasazi neighbors. It was by the process of scientific elimination, therefore, that he reached the conclusion that southwestern cannibalism "appears to have originated in Mexico, where the practice was common and dates back 2,500 years...," Turner wrote. "We speculate that this force consisted of cultists and warriors of the Quetzalcoatl-Xipe Totec-Tezcatlipoca deity complex who overwhelmed the local residents, much the way the soldiers led by Cortez fell upon Mexico. Terrorism is what we are talking about; cannibalism was the weapon that forced Chaco Canyon to be built."

He rests his case in part on the great wooden beams supporting the roofs of the large pueblos. It is believed that the beams were cut at least 50 miles away and carried by humans. "You don't haul 200,000 beams of wood voluntarily. People were coerced into producing Chaco. The only way you coerce people is through terror and power." Turner speculated in the interview, too, that workers also may have been drugged."

The questions hang in the desert air. Was it evil that caused the Great Abandonment?

Truth be known, perhaps modern day people are not supposed to know what happened at Chaco.

Let the mystery be!

ABOUT THE AUTHOR

My object in living is to unite
my avocation and my vocation.

- ROBERT FROST FROM "TWO TRAMPS IN MUDTIME"

The year was 1969. James Bishop, Jr., was a magazine correspondent on the east coast. One day a river-runner from Utah walked into his office and handed him a water-stained book. It was *Desert Solitaire*, written by a Utah/Arizona Park Ranger by the name of Ed Abbey. "Forget those documents," he said, pointing to stacks on the office floor. "Read this book, instead, if you want to know what's happening in America." Having worked for years at the center of things—or what he then thought was the center of things, Wall Street, Madison Ave, D.C.,—what need had he for such a book? Anyway, to him Utah and Arizona was just flyover country. His books included *The Consumer Revolution—Let the Seller Beware, Creating Abundance, a Different Energy Future.*

It was in 1983 that he left the East. His lovely California mother was dying. Toward the end she said that he should go to a small town in Arizona with a creek running through it. It was Sedona, he found out later, known to New Agers as anodes for the secret wires running through vortexes.

In that new place, stories filled the air. River trips rocked the soul. The days of politico/journalism faded, new doors opened, awards received, many stories accepted: *Arizona Highways*, the *Los Angeles Times*, *America West Magazine*, *High Country News*, the *Washington Post*, *Phoenix Magazine*, California Academy of Science, *Plateau Journal*, *Sedona Magazine* and the *Excentric*.

In the Southwest came the William Allen White Gold medal presented by the University of Kansas, shared with Bennie Blake; The Arizona Press Club presented him with its top award for Hogans for Hope, an account about Navajos making homes from pine logs.

No more wandering. Today he lives in the land of double rainbows near the Indian nations, in flyover country and really believes he's at the center of things. By the way, there's a water-stained copy of *Desert Solitaire*, next to his bed. His biography of Abbey is there, too.

In this place, the land and the imagination are forever merging. Humans either become part of the land, or they leave. That's how he met Walt, a 1,000-year-old Sinagua Indian skull concealed on a hill near the Verde River. "Listen to him," said the legendary boatman Parsons. "He knows the secrets."

James Bishop was educated in New England and has three children and six grandchildren.